Things I
Have
Withheld

Kei Miller

Things I Have Withheld

essays

Grove Press
New York

The following essays have been previously published in slightly altered form: An early version of "Letters to James Baldwin" was originally commissioned by Manchester Literature Festival and published in the *Manchester Review*. "The Buck, the Bacchanal, and Again, the Body" and "The White Women and the Language of Bees" previously appeared in *PREE*. "Mr Brown, Mrs White, and Ms Black" previously appeared in *Granta*.

First published in Great Britain in 2021 by Canongate Books Ltd

Published simultaneously in Canada
Printed in the United States of America

First Grove Atlantic hardcover edition: September 2021

Library of Congress Cataloging-in-Publication data is available for this title.

ISBN 978-0-8021-5895-6
eISBN 978-0-8021-5896-3

Grove Press
an imprint of Grove Atlantic
154 West 14th Street
New York, NY 10011

Distributed by Publishers Group West

groveatlantic.com

21 22 23 24   10 9 8 7 6 5 4 3 2 1

For Karen Lloyd and Jaevion Nelson
who not only say, but also do, the most important things.
With all my admiration.

Forty years ago when I was born, the question of having to deal with what is unspoken by the subjugated, what is never said to the master . . . was a very remote possibility; it was in no one's mind.

—James Baldwin, speaking at Cambridge University, 1965

CONTENTS

CONSIDERING THE SILENCE
(AN AUTHOR'S NOTE)

Consider, for a moment,

    the silence—

this terrible white

    space;

all the things

      we never say,

and why?

T his is what comes to mind when I consider the silence: how I saved my words for the stairwell in Streatham Hill, London, right outside the flat where I lived at the time; how I would sit there many nights, a little shell-shocked, and mumbling to myself.

If that sounds a bit like madness, maybe it is because that is what it was. I had ended up in a bad relationship. It was never violent but always volatile. I could never predict what would set things off—what might produce the latest bout of rage. I felt ashamed as well, to be a man such as I was, such as I am—tall and black—and so fearful of a person I was supposed to feel safe with; afraid of doing the wrong thing, and especially afraid of saying the wrong thing. Instead, I saved my words for the stairwell—rehashing arguments to myself, trying to unravel them, to understand them, and wondering how I might say things better the next time.

I was often accused of being silent, which was fair. My silence was also a strategy—a way to survive. Whenever I risked words—however carefully, however softly, even if it was just to answer the innocuous question, "How are you feeling?"—it could be met with such an explosive tantrum that I quickly learned to rarely take the risk. The specifics of that experience were new to me; I had never been in a relationship like it before. My reaction, however—the way I responded—was familiar. It was an old habit. Sitting on that stairwell at nights only emphasised what had always been true for me—that the moments when I am most in need of words are exactly the moments when I lose faith in them, and when I fall back into silence.

I suspect it is the same for a great many of us. We keep things to ourselves. We withhold them because of fear—because those things that we need to say, or acknowledge, or confess, or our own failings that we need to own up to—they can feel so important, it is hard to trust them to something so unsafe as words.

The essays that follow are not about the awful relationship, but they are about things I have withheld. The book's title is one that I have borrowed from the poet, Dionne Brand—something she once said at the beginning of one of her own essays, and which I find myself pondering over and over, the way she connects her own body to the bodies of others and the silence between:

> Some part of this text we are about to make is already written . . . for that I am a black woman speaking to a largely white audience is a major construction of the text. Blackness and Whiteness structure and mediate our interchanges—verbal, physical, sensual, political—they mediate them so that there are some things that I will say to

you and some things that I won't. And quite possibly the most important things will be the ones that I withhold.

Each of these essays is an act of faith, an attempt to put my trust in words again. They are attempts to offer, at long last, a clearer vocabulary to the things I only ever mumbled, at night, sitting there on an outside stairwell in Streatham Hill, London.

I

LETTERS TO JAMES BALDWIN

Dear James,

I wish I could call you Jimmy, the way that woman you described as handsome and so very clever—Toni Morrison—always called you Jimmy, which meant that she loved you, and you her, and that in the never-ending Christmas of your meetings (this is how she described it) you sat, both of you, in the same room, the ceiling tall enough to contain your great minds, drinking wine or bourbon and talking easily about this world. I wish that I could sit with you now and talk that easy talk about difficult things—the kind of talk that includes our shoulders, and our hands on each other's shoulders, the way we touch each other, unconsciously, as if to remind ourselves of our bodies and that we exist in this world. But here is the rub, this awful fact—that you do not exist in this world, not any more—at least, not your body; only your body of work, and I can only write back to that and to the name that attached itself to those words rather than the name that attached itself to your familiar body. Not Jimmy then, but James—a single syllable that conjures up kings and Bibles—appropriate in its own way, except it does not conjure your shoulders or your hands which I imagine as warm and which I never knew but somehow miss, and I am writing to you now with the hope that you might help me.

Dear James,

I read your review of Langston Hughes. "Every time I read [him]," you wrote, "I am amazed all over again by his genuine gifts—and depressed that he has done so little with them." "The poetic trick," you went on to say, moving from review to sermon (because there was never a pulpit you could refuse, and never a pulpit you did not earn), "is to be within the experience and outside it at the same time." You thought Hughes failed because he could only ever hold the experience outside, and you understood the why of this—the experiences that we must hold outside ourselves if we are ever to write them and not be broken by them.

But you were never able to do that. You were never able to write anything that did not implicate your own body.

James, here is a truth: I do not think much of your poems, and I suspect you will not think that a cruel way to start this exchange, and that it says more about me and my insecurities that I must begin in this way of making you fallible, approachable. To read you as I have been reading you all these years is, quite frankly, to encounter majesty—something enthroned, something that can only be approached on one's knees, with one's eyes trained to the floor. I know that image would bring you no comfort or pride, to have a black man so stooped, so lowered before you. Forgive me then my truth. I read *Jimmy's Blues* and was struck by your genuine gifts and how little you had made of them.

That isn't really fair. I know. You had never tried seriously to be a poet. *Jimmy's Blues* was more our collection than it was yours—just our own desperate attempt to read something new from you, to find once again in your words some shard of beauty and truth. So we gathered together the few poems you had written—one here, one there—and put them together in a book you had never imagined. And the thing is this: the beauty was there, the elegance of thought we have come to expect from you—but the beauty was cumulative, a result of the whole poem and not of its individual parts. You were always poetic but you weren't quite a poet—though you could have been. You could have been amazing. You didn't know how to pack enough into that most basic unit of poetry— the line.

What Hughes had, and what I think you lacked, James, was an instinctive understanding of the form of poetry, of the lyric line and what could be contained in it, and how that line might break and how it might take its breath. But I think if you and Langston Hughes were one person, James Hughes maybe, or Langston Baldwin, if such a person had written poetry—poems in which the body was present and vulnerable, and that broke in the same soft places where lines break—I think I would not have survived. I think I would have read such poetry and not been able to breathe.

Dear James,

I think about why we write letters—as an antidote to distance, as a cure for miles and the spaces that stretch between us. *If the beloved were present, there would be no need to write.* I think about the distance that is between us, which is only the distance of life and death and nothing more, because (and this is painful to say) there is little between the world you described, the set of circumstances you wrote of, and the set of circumstances we live in now. And what I want from you is a way—a way to write the things I have been trying so hard to write.

James, I do not think much of your poetry, but I think everything of your essays and it is essays that I have been trying to write but have stopped and need your help. What you had and what I lack is an instinctive under-standing of the form—the sentence that you could make as clear as glass, style whose purpose was only ever to show and never to obscure—and how you could write these things that were so muscular and so full of grace is a wonder to me.

The essays I've been writing—they began because of something Dionne Brand once wrote about "the most important things". She suggested the most important things are, in fact, the things we almost never say, because of fear, or because we think they can only be said at the cost of friendships. I have been wondering how to say them.

"We still live, alas, in a society mainly divided into black and white. Black people still do not, by and large, tell white people the truth and white people still do not want to hear the truth." Oh James . . . ain't that the goddamn truth!

James, there are still men who wear white sheets in that country to which you were born, and who burn crosses and who march in support of the Aryan nation. There are still men who tattoo Nazi signs onto their skulls, and people who spit at me and call me nigger. I have no desire to write to such people, to condemn them, because that kind of racism, that kind of hatred is so unimaginative, so obviously deprived of reason and morality that why I should waste words or intellect on it is strange to me.

But the big, terrible things distract us from the other things, which are both smaller and more urgent, and prevent us from loving or trusting each other. I think about why I write essays—as an antidote to distance, as a cure to what stretches between my best self and my worst self, or between my friends, however close we are—the people I laugh with, the aunts who I kiss, the men I have kissed, the people I love, the people who want to be good people, who try every day to be good people, to do good things, but how so often between us, between our love is this black and white world, these truths that, by and large, I do not say and by God, we do not want to hear.

Dear James,

It is the body that I wish to write about—these soft houses in which we live and in which we move and from which we can never migrate, except by dying. I want to write about our bodies, and what they mean, and how they mean, and how those meanings shift even as our bodies move throughout the world, throughout time and space.

I do not often like to think about my own body, or even look at it. Left to itself, my body relishes in fatness and a general lack of definition, though this is not true at the present moment. At the present moment my body is hard and muscled because I have been swimming and going to the gym and running and trying hard to undo the things that my body would rather do. I look in the mirror now and wonder how long this new shape will last. I do not like to talk about my body, because I might have to talk about its weight, or else the weight of my insecurities. But I must talk about it, because it has meant so many things in so many places.

At an immigration desk in Iraq, before boarding the plane that will take me away, I am pointed towards a small room. I cannot remember much about that room now—if there were windows or if there was a ceiling fan, its slow blades uselessly stirring the warm air. This is what comes to my mind now—a windowless room and a useless ceiling fan, though I am not confident in the memory. In the small room I am ordered to take off all my clothes. I fear that they will put on latex gloves, that they will put a finger inside my body searching for drugs. They will not find any. I wonder when it was that Iraq became a popular departure point for drug mules, but I do not wonder what it is about my body that has aroused suspicion. I am used to it. I am used to being pointed to small rooms. I am used to being interrogated again, and again, and again. But I've never been asked to strip before. I stand there with my trousers and my underwear pooled around my ankles. I am aware of the pudginess of my belly, aware of my penis, unimpressive in its flaccidity, aware of a bead of sweat that has escaped the pit of my arm and is now running down my side. They sit—three men in uniform—and silently observe my body, and suddenly this does not surprise me either.

All week in Erbil, I had been literally chased by men as I walked along the streets. It had scared me at first—seeing them lift up their thawbs like modest British women from the nineteenth century and run towards me. What seemed threatening at first was usually defused when they handed me their phones and through a series of gestures, a sort of sign language, made me know that they only wanted a picture. A picture with me and my strange body. So here, in this small room, it does not surprise me that these officials who have the power to stop me, who have the power to order me into a small room, who have the power to order me to take off all my clothes, have done that. They have ordered me to strip and they do nothing more than observe my body for a minute or two and then they tell me to put my clothes back on and leave.

I am always being stopped. In New Zealand, in Dubai, in France, in Miami, I am stopped. The officers have looked carefully from my passport and then to my face, and all the time assessing me, sizing me up, and my body—this body that must be spoken about—this body that in some contexts arouses suspicion, and in other contexts, lust, in others anger, in others curiosity—this body that has meant such different things to such different people—I must talk about it, and about its meanings.

James, I must talk about my body as black, and my body as male, and my body as queer. I must talk about how our bodies can variously assume privilege or victimhood from their conflicting identities. I do not want to talk about racists or classists or sexists because most people in the world do not assume themselves to be these things. I do not assume them about myself. And yet I know we participate in them all the same—in racism and classism and sexism. We participate with the help of our bodies, or because of our bodies—because our bodies have meanings we do not always consider.

Dear James,

I am writing this letter from an airport in Florida, an airport named after the city which it serves, but which you must not confuse for that city. Airports seem to be their own places and never really a part of the cities that claim them. There is such a keen sense, as there is in hospitals—of formality, sterility and limbo—of not being in a place but being between places, of being in a space between the life where you were and the life that you are heading to. I am always in airports, in this strange collection of wings and tarmac and glass doors and duty-free shops.

It is at Tallahassee Airport that you describe the meeting of a woman with her chauffeur—the meeting between a white woman and a black man, and what could pass as friendliness if we did not know any better, if we did not know the codes that allow, and the codes that forbid, and the lines that must never be crossed.

"If she were smiling at me that way," you write, "I would expect to shake her hand. But if I should put out my hand, panic, bafflement, and horror would then overtake that face, the atmosphere would darken, and danger, even the threat of death, would immediately fill the air."

James—this is what happened: on my first day in my present job I arrived early, in the dark, before the bird had sung its first song. I was now a full-fledged professor, which seemed to me a spectacular thing, being some years shy of forty, and being, of course, black. And so I was there in my office, but it was so very early, and it was my first day. It took me by surprise when the door began to jiggle, though it seemed to take the cleaning lady by much greater surprise to find someone present after she entered. She took one look at me, screamed and ran away. And James, I didn't even think much of that—I shrugged, and thought in time we would meet officially and laugh at this first bizarre interaction—but soon there was a loud rapping on the door. I opened it to campus security, burly men talking brusquely into their walkie-talkies—*We have arrived at the scene*, they reported to some disembodied voice of authority on the other end. I had to present IDs and photographs to explain the spectacle of my body in this space, to prove that I had every right to be there. And how our titles meant nothing in that moment. I was no longer a professor and the woman a cleaning lady—I was just a black man, and she a white woman, and my presence had terrified her. These were the same old Black Codes being enforced, in which black people had to produce ID papers to explain themselves, our spectacular presences in places we are not easily imagined. But I had no way to say any of this, James—to talk about this history that had become so painfully present, and how we all played our roles so brutally, so perfectly. I could not tell them how you had already imagined this moment at an airport in Tallahassee, the panic, the bafflement, the horror—the sense of danger that can suddenly fill the air.

Dear James,

I have grown so weary of intentions—the claiming of them, and the denial of them. *I did not intend to be racist,* they say to me all the time. *He did not intend to be racist. If there is no intention, how can it be racist?* They ask me again and again. They mean it to be rhetorical. They think the logic is so devastatingly simple and clear that it cannot be answered, but it is only that I have grown weary. As if one could say, *It was an accident! I did not intend to push you to the floor, and so the pain that you claim to feel shooting up your back cannot be real. It cannot be real because I did not intend it.* And I wonder especially when white women proffer such logic or ask such questions—when they say how can it be racist if there was no intention. Because I imagine these same women would flinch if a strange man were to call them honey, and ask them what they were doing out without their husbands. I imagine these women would rightly call such a man out on his sexism and would sneer if he said, *But I did not intend to be sexist! I love women! How can I be sexist?*

James, this is what happened: An old woman was outside my flat. She looked disoriented and an overwhelming feeling of helplessness emanated from her. She was babbling to herself and looking hopefully into the faces of many passers-by. They did not see her, or if they did, they ignored her. I suspected she had dementia or Alzheimer's. I could not know for sure, but I thought of my own grandfather in the midst of one of his episodes, how he had walked away from the house in Red Hills, Jamaica, and then miles and miles through Kingston. For days we could not find him. I considered the old woman, and though she was white and though she was a woman, she reminded me now of my grandfather lost in his own city and in his own mind. I knew there was little I could do for her, but I could not walk away. I touched her gently on the shoulder. "Do you need any help?"

She looked up then and when her eyes found my face she gasped and clutched her heart. "Oh my god!" she exclaimed, reminding me of my body and what my body meant in a city like London. Suddenly it seemed the passers-by, who had been ignoring the old woman before, were not ignoring her any more. I stood there, feeling accused by them all, as if I was harassing her. I walked away quickly. I left her to be lost in her own city and in her own mind.

I go to the computer and write all of this in a post. Messages start pouring in. There is a throng of responses and it is almost frightening the way these are neatly divided. My black friends respond with an all-too-knowing, *yeah, we've been there.* My white friends are both defensive and accusatory.

> . . . *But was she being racist? How do you know she was being racist?*
> . . . *Racist? But I didn't even use that word. I've just described a thing that happened to me.*
> . . . *Yes, but you're clearly implying that she is racist, and you don't know! You are a writer! You must be careful with your words. You don't know anything about her! Maybe she had a horrible experience before with a black man.*

Their sympathies seem to lie very clearly with the old woman, and so I turn off the computer. I turn it off so that once again I won't feel as if I were back out there on the streets, the passers-by all looking at me again, accusing me of my frightening height, my frightening maleness, my frightening blackness. The next morning, I see that more has been written on the thread but interestingly, not by my black friends. My black friends have become silent. Theirs is not the silence of acceptance, but it is a silence we are used to. It is the silence in which we have learned to keep our hurt because so often we are told we have no right to it, or that to even describe the hurt is irresponsible. It is the silence in which so many important things are kept.

Dear James,

In your essay, "The White Man's Guilt"—this is how you begin: "I have often wondered, and it is not a pleasant wonder, just what white Americans talk about with one another."

Haven't we all, James! Aren't we always suspicious of the conversations that our bodies prevent, that stop when we enter a room or that never get started because we are there—and how hard it is to live in this world feeling the weight of words—of ghost words that we almost never hear aloud, but are only ever suspicious of—because they exist on the edge of the other things that our friends say?

James, this is what happened: in the Caribbean, a woman from England, a friend of sorts, who is really very clever and has championed the books of many writers of colour is on a stage talking. Her interlocutor is a mutual friend. They talk about writing and life and advocacy in the way old friends do. The woman from England then says she is about to share a story, and at first she was a little worried because it is a little risqué, but then hell! It's the Caribbean. So who cares? And there was a moment, James, when everyone in the audience sighed collectively, even if not audibly. And we turned to look at each other as if to confirm—did she really just say that? She did, didn't she? Of course, we didn't care that the story was risqué, but we cared about this imagining of our home as a place without morals or values, and where anything is allowed. But we would have let it pass the way we always do—the way we have learned to brush such careless statements aside. But there was a pause on stage, and the pause was so terrifying for all of us, because we understood it and what was being contemplated. The interlocutor was biting her lip, and looking at her hands and the pause stretched and I think, in the audience—I do not know why—we were all willing her to just let it go, and we were all willing her to go there. She looked up from her hands and said, "But what exactly do you mean by that?"

We held our breaths then. We were so stunned. And I think maybe the English woman had had one too many glasses of rum punch, or maybe she was just nervous, but her words are pouring out now, and they are so careless and they are so clumsy and they do not help. And then comes another question about something else, and another question, and every question is devastating, and every answer is awful. And I find myself wondering about the quality of light that shines in the Caribbean and if it was helping me then to see things more clearly—helping me to see what had always been problematic and patronising in my friend's politics and in her advocacy. It was such a small throwaway comment she had made. It's the Caribbean, so who cares? But it was like a loose thread that unravelled the entire cardigan of her thoughts.

The conversation unspools. The questions dig deeper, they are sharper, more penetrating, as if these are questions the interlocutor had always wanted to ask but hadn't because she had been afraid, or because she thought they could only ever be asked at the cost of friendship, or because she knew they could never be answered. The woman's face is now red. Though she is trying to smile and to be composed, her eyes are trying not to water, her lips not to tremble at what I think must feel like a betrayal, like ungratefulness—these truths that people of colour almost never say, these things which her very advocacy makes possible, but which she didn't want to hear after all.

Finally, it is over. Finally, she walks off the stage and comes directly to me. "Can you believe that?" she says, in a voice both hushed and urgent, almost a hiss, but I do not know how to respond. I do not know how to offer comfort.

The next day arrives as all days arrive in the Caribbean, with boats of fishermen silent across the waters, and with parrots loud in the sky. It is another day and over breakfast the woman from England is speaking to another friend, another white woman. Her eyes dart about the room and she speaks in a conspiratorial voice. "Can we go shopping together?" she says. "I just want to be able to talk without being so goddamn careful!" And I'm not sure why, months later, the confidante tells me about this breakfast conversation, except maybe she no longer wants to be complicit in this thing, this thing that you wondered about, James, this thing that we know, that our bodies prevent conversations that hurt us even when we are not around to hear them.

Dear James,

It is always the body that I return to, our bodies and their various meanings, even though we would like to be just human—just that and nothing more, but we aren't there yet. I think about the little boy—I imagine him as three years old—who balls up his fists and ineffectively hits his father; this little boy who, in this moment, in his tiny rage, is just human, unsure of how to contain his anger at the world in his small body. And I think about his father who balls up his fists and hits his three-year-old son—and how it is the same emotion, but because his body is different it means differently. The child is not an abuser, but the father is, because his body is different—and I think about these things every day when a man says, "But why is that sexist? A woman would do it too!" Or when a white friend says, "But why is that racist? My black friends say the same things!" Or when my American friends say, "But why is that exceptionalist or fascist? People from every country feel the same way about their countries!"

And I say it is because of our bodies; it is because there are histories that haunt our bodies.

Dear James,

I think I am writing these letters to say that I resent your dying—I resent the absence of your shoulders and your hands in this world. I resent the absence of your body, even though I am grateful for the body of work. It is just that I cannot say things any better than you have, I cannot think more graciously than you have, but the world and the circumstances that you wrote to, they are still here—obstinate world that we have—as if your words did not unravel the things they should have, did not bring down the walls of Jericho, which means we who are left behind must try to write with as much grace and as much love and as much truthfulness as you taught us. But some days I resent this—I resent what you require from us, which is nothing less than what you required from yourself. My dear James, I need your help.

MR BROWN, MRS WHITE
AND MS BLACK

Mr Brown

And because high school boys had learned the habit of addressing each other and identifying themselves by their surnames, he has carried this into adulthood. He will often introduce himself simply as "Brown". "Good evening," he might say, "I am Brown." And this has become a sort of unwitting joke—for the word "brown" on the island signified something more than just a name, but a sort of ethnicity, a mulatto-ness if you will. "Brown by name and nature, I see!" is a rejoinder with which Sebastian Brown has become all too familiar. These days he even anticipates it, but is generous enough to smile each time, as if he is hearing the witticism for the first time.

When he is alone, as he is now, Mr Brown likes to think about his "brownness" though he does not share these thoughts with anyone. He learned a long time ago—from his days in college—that to share one's thoughts can be dangerous. And in any case he is not an argumentative man, nor the kind who takes much pleasure in bringing people around to his way of seeing things. It is satisfaction enough for him to live with a thought, even for years, slowly peeling away at its levels of complexity. Many evenings you will find him here—silent on the verandah that overlooks the city of Kingston, sitting with a bottle of Red Stripe, and with his thoughts.

Having travelled around the world, Mr Brown has come to the conclusion that he is a man of indeterminable race. He has seen the look of confusion on people's faces—a confusion that gives way even to an annoyance. It is as if people believe it is his own duplicitousness, his own guile and cunning that make him not reveal his true racial self to them. He wonders if such people believe that if they only knew what exactly he was, that they would then know everything about him? He knows too well the furrowed brow and how the lips of a person will part slowly, carefully, before asking him the same old question: *What exactly are you?*

When he travels through Miami he has learned to say very quickly, "No entiendo español." before they take him as Latino. In Spain he is taken as Spanish, and in Trinidad as well, though "Spanish" in Trinidad means something else. In Greece he is taken as Greek, and in Egypt and Morocco and Algeria he is taken as Arab. It is impossible for him to learn how to say "I do not understand" in every language, or "I am not this thing you think I am." In Jamaica, however, he is simply "brown" and it is a strange comfort to Sebastian, to be so placed and in a category that he knows, and understands, and accepts.

It is true, though, that some days Mr Brown thinks he may as well be Arab, or Latino, or Spanish or whatever the hell it is people think he might be. For what is race anyway but a decision that other people make about you—an assignment that has been given to you? Race, it seems to Mr Brown, is not so much what you are, as it is what people have decided that you are—what it is they see in you, how they make sense of you. Race and ethnicity are not the same things. Ethnicity is what is in your actual DNA, your genes, your ancestry and all of that. Race, on the other hand, is how society constructs you—and it does not matter whether they see wrongly or not. What they see does not need your approval, or to be corroborated by facts. For most people in the world, their ethnicity and their racial assignments are one and the same thing, so it is easy to confuse the two. For people like Mr Brown, however, things are more complicated. As Mr Brown has travelled around the world he has also travelled in and out of races.

Sebastian Brown is not always a fan of academic language, though he was once a member of the academe. He left that life many years ago and has not looked back. But sometimes, he must confess, that oh-so-turgid language actually gets things right. He is therefore a fan of the word "racialised". He believes it is altogether more accurate to say that "So-and-So is racialised as black", than to say "So-and-So *is* black". Or it is better to say, "So-and-So is racialised as white", than to say, "So and So *is* white". Sebastian Brown's mother, for instance, had always been racialised as black, though this was not the entire truth of her ethnicity, of her very mixed heritage. Her physiognomy and complexion showed little evidence of the Lebanese/Chinese/Scottish mix that was also part of her family's story and which her siblings (to her great resentment) showed off generously in the olive colour of their skin and the curly bounce of their hair. In the presence of her siblings people would ask incredulously, "Then you really have the same mother and father?" and then to themselves exclaim, "Then is how she come out so black?" In vain, Sebastian's mother had lived her life trying to insist she was more than what her skin suggested. "I'm not really black you know! On my mother's side, my grandfather did come to Jamaica straight from Lebanon—set up shop right there on King's Street, and my father's mother was a woman who did mix with Chinese and white—no nayga was in her at all!" It didn't matter—this useless insisting on genealogy. She came out looking the way she did and was always racialised as black.

All that complicated genealogy was only stored up inside her to be passed down to her children—her children whose brownness she would revel in, taking it as new evidence of her own superior pedigree. Over and over, his mother had said to her two children, "Look at your clear skin, and your good hair. We are people of a higher calibre. Remember that!" And these were things said so matter-of-factly, and corroborated by everyone—by teachers, by friends, by security guards who dutifully opened every gate wide for them—that it was difficult for Sebastian Brown to unlearn these things. How does one unlearn privilege, especially the kind that is given to you daily and without question, so it does not seem like privilege at all but simply the everyday-ness of life?

At Harvard he had studied economics. He had even begun a PhD, though his heart had never been in it. He was clever enough and had won a scholarship. It was the 1990s. His group of friends were mostly international students and he had envied the way they were not only bright, but also eager.

It was as if they all wanted to change the world. They truly believed that they would. Deconstruction theory was all the rage then, and having come from small corners of the world, they were also postcolonialists—in love with Said and Spivak and Bhabha. It was at dinner one evening that Prisha, a linguist from India, had asked him, "So, how does postcolonial theory inform your own work as an economist?" The whole table had turned to him, for he had not really spoken about his work before, his research, his ideas. They were very curious. But Sebastian Brown was not like them. He did not believe in things in the way they did. He didn't have the same kind of passion. He had raised his eyes querulously. "The postcolonial?" he'd asked. "Is that a real thing? Isn't it just a category of discrimination that rich kids from the third world like to claim when we find ourselves here, in America, in the academy, and we want tenure or something like that? It's nice to feel oppressed. Then we don't have to face the fact that back home we are actually the oppressors."

You could have heard a mouse fart! He'd tried to take it back, to laugh awkwardly as if it was just a joke, but everyone could see it wasn't a joke at all. It was a statement so profoundly unfair, and yet so profoundly true. He had betrayed them. In the silence that followed he could already feel the tenuous knots of friendship unravelling—people pulling away from him. He had revealed too much of their selves to their selves, and perhaps too much of himself—for there it was—what no one had been able to read in him before, because they had had no context to read it—his sense of his Jamaican brownness—a privilege which not even America could diminish in him.

He never finished the PhD. He left—ABD—All But Dissertation. He has never regretted that, though some days, back in Jamaica, he thinks maybe he should have studied something else—something like sociology, or even ethnography. Lord knows he spends enough of his spare time thinking about these things. He has collected old "casta" charts from Mexico—read their explanations of mulatto, quadroon, octoroon, mestizo, mustee, zambo. When he hears new racial terms across the Caribbean, he writes these down as well—dougla, hawkwei, shabine. The distinctions within a single racial category also fascinate him: busha—a white native; whitey—a white tourist; red—which could just as easily be one of those German-descended creoles from St Elizabeth, or a poor white who had been burned red from the sun.

Still, it is brownness that most fascinates Mr Brown—the way it both functions as a race—as its own distinct race—and yet is hidden as a racial category. Sometimes this is quite obvious, like when the brown woman down the road got herself into that great big deal of trouble. She had made a public complaint about her neighbour—her neighbour who happened to be a black man—her neighbour who was really just a country boy who had done well for himself, had come into money and moved himself into the well-heeled neighbourhood. She had complained, as uptown people will, that his music was too loud, and that his parties were too many and that they went on well into the morning. And even on Sundays there was no respite, for he would rev his motorbike along the once-quiet street. It had all become too much for her. He was a terror. And how she wished and wished and wished (this is what she wrote) that he would just go back to where he came from.

Poor brown lady. She had taken him as just another country boy—the kind of boy she had learned her whole life that she should be able to talk down to and reprimand. She did not take him for who he had become, a man beloved around the world, the decorated Olympian, Usain Bolt. The backlash was tremendous. Some people thought she would have to migrate. It got worse as the story emerged from other neighbours that his parties were actually not that many, and his music not so loud, and though he did ride a motorbike, so did several others in the neighbourhood—but these other motorcycle riders looked very much like the woman who was complaining. They did not look like Usain Bolt. So why did she zero in on him? Why?

But here is what Mr Brown finds fascinating, here is the real rub of it—that when the brown lady was accused of being out of order, the entire country agreed, *Oh yes! Yes! De woman was well outa order!* And when she was accused of being unfair, and rude, and classist, everyone was hollering as if they were at a political rally, blowing their vuvuzelas to punctuate every point. *Is true! Is true! She too raaas unfair, and she bloodclawt rude, and she look down pon poor people like she better dan we.* But then, when someone introduced that big and contentious R word—when it was suggested that in addition to her general rudeness, and her classism, that as well her statement was racist, then all at once the same critics were sputtering out their cups of tea, turning to each other frantically, raising their hands and shouting together, "Stop! Stop! Stop! Now this thing is going too far!"

It was the same old Sankey after that: Yes, we have a class problem in Jamaica. Of course we do. And as well, there is a colour problem—so many people bleaching their skin. It is an issue. You might even go so far as to say we have a problem with shadeism or colourism, but no one can accuse us of having a race problem! And look at this case in particular. The lady is brown! Do you understand that? She is brown! That means there is some black in her. Somewhere. The point is, she cannot possibly be racist.

It seems to Mr Brown that brownness is like a magical cloak in Jamaica, how the person who wears it is allotted a kind of power and prestige but when push comes to shove, that same cloak can hide the wearer within blackness or even whiteness.

Mr Brown understands his island's reluctance to use the big and contentious R word. It is a brutal word, uncouth even in the softness of its own sounds. And it is generally assumed that racism is a thing that only happens on TV, or in America, or in the distant past, and it is always tied to white supremacy. Mr Brown thinks differently. Mr Brown believes that to understand racism, the first thing you must understand is how race is constructed and how it functions in a specific place. "White" is not the same thing everywhere, and "Black" is not the same thing everywhere, and some countries have races that do not function at all in other countries—bodies that when they travel cause people to look at them curiously, and if the onlooker is brave enough they might ask, "But exactly what are you?"

Mr Brown believes that only then—only when we know how race works in a specific place—can we begin to think about the ways in which power and prestige are distributed unevenly based on those local ideas about race and colour and phenotypical features. If race works and behaves differently in different places, then the same is true for racism. Mr Brown does not believe that the brown lady who complained about Usain Bolt was a white supremacist, or that she didn't have black friends, or black aunts and uncles and cousins. But he believes that she was participating in a kind of racism all the same—a kind of racism that is specific to Jamaica but for which the island does not yet have the language to talk about or examine.

But Mr Brown only thinks these thoughts. He would never share them with anyone, because these are the kinds of thoughts that implicate him. And why would he want to do that?

His phone buzzes. He glances at the screen and sees that it is an incoming WhatsApp message from his neighbour, Mrs Veronica White. Instinctively, he looks across to the property next door and sure enough there she is on her own verandah. She smiles and waves in his direction. He reads the message. "If you are walking over to no. 18 later, do knock on my gate. I will walk over with you." He had almost forgotten about the dinner party. He looks back over and gives Mrs White the thumbs up sign.

Mrs White

And because she has developed this kind of relationship with
Marva, where the housekeeper is so at ease with her employer
(or at least, so it would seem to Mrs White) that strange things
occasionally fly out of her mouth, it is Marva who said to her
one afternoon as she dusted the family photographs arranged
on the wall of the living room, "But you know, what I really
don't understand, ma'am, is how oonoo manage fi stay white.
For it don't have so many white people in Jamaica like it did
have one time, but is like oonoo still manage fi find each
other, and oonoo manage fi stay as white as the driven snow
itself, even here in this great big sea of black."

And because it was not really a question, and because even
if it had been, there was no real answer that Mrs White could
have given (this freedom to speak openly not being accorded
as equally to the employer as it was to the employee) all Mrs
White could say was "Hm," the smallest sound of acknowledgement. A part of her wanted to laugh, though. What the
hell did Marva know about "driven snow", and was she as
white as all that? This is the first part of the answer she might
have given Marva—that in fact her whole family had not
stayed white, and some had never been white to begin with.
But if Mrs White had said anything of the sort, Marva would
have immediately reexamined the pictures on the walls; she
would have flipped through the family albums—she would
have observed all the fair shades of skin, all the straight or
curly hair on top of everyone's heads, their grey, and blue and

light-brown eyes, and she would have sucked her teeth loudly. "Which one of dem not white, ma'am?" "Jamaican White", after all, was its own thing. Mrs White understands this much.

And so, over time, she has thought about it. Really—how had her family managed to stay white? Was it, as Marva seemed to think, that they had some inner radar, some beacon that sought out the few other white people on the island? No. It wasn't that exactly. Mrs White thinks of the men and women who have married into her family and how they have come from everywhere—not just Jamaica. They have come from Barbados, and Trinidad, and St Vincent, and quite a few from the United States. It was not so much whiteness that they were drawn to but, ironically, its opposite—the ability to not see whiteness at all. In her early days, Mrs White found she could only ever be intimate with a man who was able to see beyond her colour and race—a man who could see her simply as a person. The truth is, it usually took a white man to do that.

She cannot say to Marva the truth—that it is so very hard to be a white person in Jamaica. Marva would simply say, "Hm," the smallest of sounds, but in that smallness would have been a world of rebuke. *Hard, ma'am? You know bout hard life? You think you really know nothing bout what is hard, living as you do way up on this hill?* Mrs White would not have been able to compete, so she keeps these thoughts to herself. There are so many truths she has had to keep to herself.

But the truth is, it was hard being white. It is hard for Mrs White to walk into every goddamn room and have every goddamn person decide immediately that they understood everything there was to understand about her—and more than that, they would have decided that she in turn could not possibly understand anything about them, and about their lives. It was in high school that Mrs White had become truly white. It was a traumatic experience. Back then, before she was Mrs Veronica White—she had been Veronica Levy—a shy young thing in love with Nancy Drew books. She had attended a very good high school in Kingston. They were all such privileged children at that school—not a one of them wanting for money. Their parents were doctors, lawyers, High Court judges, owners of stores in the Half Way Tree plazas. Race wasn't a big thing until the history classes started. It wasn't that anyone had been ignorant of the history of Jamaica—the whole terrible lot of it—chattel slavery, English landlords, Scottish overseers, the brutal labour it took to work the sugarcane fields, the whips, the great houses, the rebellions, the indentured Indians and Chinese. Veronica at least had known it all before, but never before had she sat in a class with someone like Bobby McKenzie.

Now that she is a grown woman, Mrs White can look back at that time and dismiss Bobby McKenzie as just another cruel child, the way that children in school are so often cruel. He was a boy who took special pleasure in tormenting other students—and possibly, he was infatuated with her but knew no other way to show it. He started calling her Missus, or M'Lady, or even Buckra. The other students squealed with laughter at these jibes, and then took them up as well. These were her new names—never Veronica, but Buckra, Missus, or M'Lady, as if suddenly she was nothing more than the colour of her skin.

When Bobby McKenzie sat behind her in class, he would flick rubber bands at her. They stung. When she cried out or complained, he would say wickedly, "That's nothing compared to the whip, M'Lady." Bobby McKenzie was a bully, and it had not occurred to Veronica in those days that all he could accuse her of being was white. He could not accuse her of having money because his family had more. His father owned one of the biggest haberdashery stores on the island, and she had heard it from reliable sources that in their backyard the McKenzies had a swimming pool the size of a small lake.

Those were hard days for Veronica. She often took the hurt from school home with her. Mr Levy had tried to comfort his daughter. "Look, this is the country you were born to, and you will just have to learn how to survive it. It isn't easy for anybody here. It not easy for black people, and despite what people will tell you it, it not so easy for white people either. But you just have to find your own way to survive it."

"And if you don't find a way to survive it?" she had asked.

Her father had only said, "Hm," the smallest of sounds. He had made the sound because he thought there was no need to answer the question; they already knew the answer. It was the 1970s. White families were leaving Jamaica week after week to settle in countries where they could simply be people—where no one looked on their whiteness as the be-all and end-all of who they were. Veronica had been going with her father and mother to Norman Manley Airport almost every other week, standing on the waving gallery to bid good-bye to some aunt, some cousin, some neighbour, climbing the metal stairs and into the belly of the beast, never to be seen again. If you didn't find a way to survive, this is who you would become. You would become someone who left. Mr Levy did not want his daughter to leave. He did not want his white Jamaican family to be *that* kind of white Jamaican family. So he looked his daughter in the eyes, deciding that she deserved more than just a "Hm".

"I will say it again: this is your country too. And every one of us have to reckon with how it became our country—this messed-up little island. But is your country all the same. You don't have any other but this. So don't make nobody take that from you. You hear me?"

Sometimes Marva has responded to one of Mrs White's questions with: "Ma'am, story deh fi talk, but bench nuh deya fi siddung pon." She says this when Mrs White has tried to use her as a sort of native informant and Marva has decided that the answer—the story—is too long, too complex, and she doubts that Mrs White will ever understand it. Mrs White might ask, "Marva, why so much gunfights happen in your old neighbourhood?" or "Marva, why all those boys on the street corner bleaching their good good skin?" And Marva says, "Ma'am, story deh fi talk, but bench nuh deya fi siddung pon." Well, this is exactly how Mrs White feels about Marva's comment, "How oonoo manage fi stay white?" Marva, she wants to say, there is a story I could tell you, but there is no bench long enough for us to sit down together.

But if there existed such a bench—such a place of understanding between the two women—then Mrs White would have told Marva about all the Bobby McKenzies she has met in her life, men who seemed to make it their duty to make her feel bad about herself, who sometimes with just a look, a sneer, dismissed her or accused her of such terrible things. Although she knew she wanted to marry a Jamaican man, she knew it could never be that kind of man—a man who would notice her whiteness and make her feel bad about it. She thought she had been lucky to find such a man, but she is old enough now to know that it wasn't luck at all. It was simply what she thought she needed from the world and the world had provided. Mr White is the father of her children; for this she will always be thankful. But that dirty, skirt-chasing infidel is long gone out of her life. Divorced. She is thankful for that as well.

And if there was a bench long enough, Mrs White might have risked another truth with Marva. She might have said: *Marva, to tell you the God's honest truth, some days I think it would have been better if I had had my children with a black man. At least then they would have come out brown, and life could have been a little easier for them.*

Oh the 70s! All those trips to the airport. All that waving people off from the waving gallery. Black Power had changed so many things on the island; white people no longer sat comfortably on top of the totem pole, but black people hadn't replaced them. That was the sad thing. Brown people had.

Mrs White loves her children as they are. Of course she does. But she would be lying if she didn't admit to having entertained this strange thought—wishing them a little darker. She wonders though if Marva would have loved her children any more or any less if they had been any other colour? Sometimes it has seemed that Marva loves the two children the way a little black girl might love her white dolly. It concerns Mrs White how fiercely protective Marva has been of the two children, but she does not want to seem ungrateful. It's just that some days the fierceness of Marva's love seems to echo the exact history that Mrs White does not like to consider. Still, she has benefited from Marva's love in ways she will never be able to repay.

When Alexandria was just sixteen years old, a boy had driven her home from a party. They were just there—in his car at the gate—and it was Marva who roused herself from sleep and heard the girl whimpering for help. But how had Marva heard that? Were her ears more attuned to the sound of a woman in trouble? Mrs White doesn't know. She only feels guilty, as if that night she had failed as a mother. Marva's room was at the back of the house, not even facing the gate as Mrs White's room was. And yet, for whatever reason, Marva woke up at 2 a.m. that morning and knew that little Miss Alexandria was out there at the gate and in need of help. The boy who had dropped the young girl home had seemed so nice at first, but soon he was getting very handsy, very quickly. They had just been sitting in his car, there at the gate, talking. She was already home. He had dropped her home, so what could be dangerous now? And then his hand was on her knee which wasn't so bad until the hand began to go up her legs, and then it was pulling at her panties, and his rough fingers were trying to go inside her. She was telling him no and no and no and Kevin! Stop that! She was trying to pull the wayward hand away, and then he wasn't so nice any more. He used just one of his hands to hold onto her two, and with the other hand he went back up her legs and towards her panties and she couldn't stop him or twist away from him. And then there was Marva, like some kind of maroon warrior, like Nanny herself—wonderful Marva standing on the outside of the car with a cutlass in her hand. The boy didn't see her until Marva used the flat side of the cutlass and slapped the car window with such a ferocity one was surprised the glass didn't break. Two other car alarms went off on the street, the way the very road had shook, and the boy who was not so nice after all was suddenly screaming and jumping about the car and hit his nose against the windscreen and made it bleed. Marva was now shouting for the whole neighbourhood to hear. "Get yu nasty black hand dem off of Miss Alexandria this minute!" and then some other things, other things about his nastiness, and about his blackness, as if the two things depended on each other.

Mrs White is grateful. She is so very grateful. But weeks after, when she thinks about that night, she cannot help but think about the things that Marva said. And why did she say those things? On that night the boy had opened the car and let Alexandria out; Alexandria had run towards Marva. Mrs White who was finally awake was running towards the gate. Marva wielded her cutlass against the car a second time and it banged. The boy cowered. "Drive!" Marva shouted. "Drive yu bloodclawt car and never come back here or else a swear a kill yu mi own self. Renk and nasty lickle johncrow!"

And there it was—the fierceness of Marva's love, and her protection, but beneath it all something strange, like the sour aftertaste of history.

That was some years ago. Alexandria has now gone abroad to school. On the phone Alexandria tells her mother, "Mom, here people are always telling me that I am white, and I just tell them no, I am Jamaican." And Mrs White laughs at this, though she doesn't quite understand it. Still, she takes a deep satisfaction in the way that her daughter is claiming the island as her own. Mrs White secretly hopes that Alexandria will come back one day, and that her daughter would not turn into the kind of young woman that she was—afraid and annoyed by what people saw in her, afraid to breach the gap and tell them the most important things, and to have the most important things said back to her.

There is a pinging at the gate and Mrs White remembers, oh of course, it is Mr Sebastian Brown from next door come to accompany her. She opens the door. "I'm coming!" she calls out, and throws a scarf around her shoulders. They will only be walking three houses down the road, to no. 18—to Ms Black's house—but recently things have been so unsafe on the island that Mrs White feels much safer walking those few metres in the company of a man.

Ms Black

And because tonight she is hosting a dinner party for the neighbours, Ms Black's nightly conversation with her mother —a conversation that usually goes on for half an hour at

35

least—is cut short. "Yes Mama," she says on the phone, "I can't talk tonight because people coming over any minute. I just checking in to make sure everything all right."

"Yes chile," her mother says, and Ms Black smiles at the way in which she will always be a "child" to her mother, despite the fact that she is sixty years old. A sixty-year-old child—what a thing! "Everyting awrite," her mother continues, "though de nurse woman she just come een and gimme dem set o pink tablets that you know mi don't like. It always do something terrible to mi tummy. Now gas going to fill me up all day tomorrow. And den . . ."

"Awrite Mama," Ms Black interrupts, knowing that if she doesn't the conversation will stretch to its usual half hour. "Like I say, I can't really talk now. But make sure that you take whatever tablets it is Miss Johnson give you to take. I feel better knowing that you have gas than to think you might fall down and dead. Tomorrow we will talk more proper, OK?"

"Awrite chile. Tomorrow."

Ms Black presses "end call" and sighs with an emotion that is something like relief. Sometimes talking to her mother is dangerous business. It is a joy, but it is also a danger. Ms Black finds that she relaxes too much when she talks to her mother. She relaxes into the person she once was but cannot be again— maybe even the person she still is but cannot show to anyone. With her mother, her voice slips into a more comfortable register. Though maybe "register" is not the right word; the right word would be "language". But Ms Black has worked very hard to never use the language in which she is most comfortable. Ms Black is known to speak slowly and carefully.

It is worry that causes this. She worries over her syntax, and about how words ought to be pronounced, even simple words. She has to make sure that an unnecessary H does not slip in front of her vowels, and that she doesn't take away the H from where it in fact belongs. It is very hard—all this work, all this effort. When what she really wants to say is "Mi si de bwoy a guh dung i road," in one fluid go, with almost no pauses between the words, she has learned to say with ridiculous formality, "I saw the young man proceeding along the road."

With her mother, things are different. Her speech is different. Her mother allows her a space to relax into herself, but once relaxed, it is difficult for her to come back to the person people expect her to be. Tonight, if she speaks at length to her mother, it would be too difficult for her to return to being the kind of person who could receive her well-to-do neighbours for a dinner party.

Ms Black thinks of herself as a simple woman. This is the story she tells of herself—that she was born in a simple place and to simple people. But the world she now lives and moves in is not simple at all. She is a politician. She is a Member of Parliament and a Minister of Government. It is especially strange to Ms Black when she goes into her constituency—a constituency in which she is greatly loved and admired. She thinks of her constituency as a simple place full of simple people. She thinks of them as her people. She knows them, and their lives, and most of all, their language. But even here, amongst her people, she cannot speak their language back to them. They expect more from her. Their love and admiration of her is contingent on the fact that she was once from them, but is no longer. They love her because she has been elevated beyond them.

When Ms Black had just joined the Party, she had felt so out of place. She had not gone to university. She did not speak well. The kind brown man who was then the leader, had taken her under his wing, and had said to her, "Ms Black, if you're going to get anywhere with these people, you will have to do elocution lessons. You will have to learn to speak better." He had said that—"these people"—as if the uptown Jamaicans who surrounded them were not his people after all, as if he and Ms Black belonged to the same group. It was his special charm as a politician, to speak as if he was an outsider to the very group that shaped him. The brown man had used his own money to sign Ms Black up for the classes he promised would help her with "these people" and she is very grateful to the brown man. Over the years she has tried hard not to disappoint him, to make use of his investment, to remember the lessons she had learned. Now she speaks slowly and carefully. And yet still, they mock her.

About her neighbour, Mr Sebastian Brown, she has heard the comment—"Brown by name and nature." About herself, she has heard a variation—"Black by name, but dark by nature"—the word "dark" on the island being a synonym for "ignorant". When the island's comedians have imitated her, or when she has watched plays where a character is clearly based on her, it is always this very slow and deliberate way of speaking that they mock. The very strategy that she has used to hide what she has been told are the worst aspects of herself is the very thing that seems to expose her as a fraud.

All over the internet, there are YouTube clips of herself saying one thing or the other—saying it wrongly, or saying it in the wrong register, the wrong language, and people fall over themselves laughing. During elections it is especially difficult for Ms Black. They call her a disgrace, an embarrassment, an intellectual lightweight. Black by name, but dark by nature. It is not that Ms Black does not understand things, and their complexity, but it is not always easy for her to attach the right words to that complexity. She has to take such care and such effort with her words and sometimes that makes her thoughts seem jumbled. It is different at nights when she speaks to her mother. When she allows herself the simple joy of talking in her own language and with its own fluency, and she finds herself able to think in that vocabulary, then everything is clear to her, and she thinks she could explain the world to itself. But during the day, she is not allowed the use of this language—the language of her thoughts.

If you asked Ms Black to tell you honestly about what she has had to endure as a politician—what she has had to overcome—she will almost certainly tell you about sexism— the way in which the world she now lives and moves in has always been an all-boys' club. But she did not go to any of the island's top boys' schools—not to Wolmer's or St George's or Jamaica College or Kingston College. And also, she would tell you about classism—how being a simple woman born to simple people in a simple place was a disadvantage she had to conquer every day. But the big and contentious R word— Racism? No no no no! Ms Black would never mention it. No way. That was never part of the dynamic as she understood it. More than half of her fellow cabinet members are black. And when the brown leader who took her under his wing died, it was a black man who took over, and Jamaica loved him. And most of the women who had looked down on her her whole life—women who called her "bhutu" and "tegareg" and "virago"—most of them were black women. This was Jamaica after all. Blackness was no hurdle that you had to overcome. Blackness could not stop you from rising. But class! Oh dear lord, class! It meant everything here. This is what Ms Black believes and this is what she would tell you.

Still, sometimes she thinks about another dinner party she had hosted some years ago when her neighbour, Sebastian Brown, had had one too many glasses of red wine and he had begun speaking in a way that Ms Black had never heard him speak before. She thought it was as if he was on the phone talking to his own mother, as if he had suddenly relaxed into himself. How the conversation had gotten around to the topic of class, she doesn't quite remember, but then all intellectual and animated conversations in Jamaica eventually get around to the topic of class. Mr Brown was suddenly banging the table as if he were in parliament. "Here is the thing! Here is the thing!" he slurred, "When it comes to racism in Jamaica, it's like the most sophisticated racism in the fucking world. You could almost not see it at all. Listen man, no teacher in Jamaica is going to tell a little girl in school: come on little miss, you need to start behaving like white people. No sah! The teacher is going to say instead: you need to start behaving like a young lady. And the teacher will tell a little boy: you need to start behaving like a gentleman. And then we cuss people how them talk bad, or them look unkempt, or them acting like a bhutu—and all these things that we say every goddamn day is really the way that we have learned to say something else—that we not acting or looking or behaving white enough. You see this thing that you all calling classism —all it is, is one of the most sophisticated examples of racism in this world! The racism that we have here in Jamaica, is a racism that knows how to hide itself."

Everyone had rushed in after that to say something, and the conversation had lurched this way and that way and then sailed into a different ocean. But days after Ms Black had thought about Mr Brown's little speech. She thought about her life as a politician and all these little things she was required to do—to speak properly, to dress properly, to act properly. But what did "properly" mean? What was it based on? Or better yet, who was it based on? And Ms Black thought maybe Mr Brown was really onto something. Yet, it wasn't a thought that she could entertain for very long. That kind of thought was dangerous thinking for a politician—for a woman in her position. She was a black woman in a black country, and that had worked to her advantage. That worked especially during elections. But when the election was over, then she would have other work to do. The people who elected her were black people, but the circles she had to move in after were oftentimes white circles or brown circles, and she could not afford to have any opinion or to share any kind of thought that accused these people—these people whose patronage she needed. She could not risk upsetting them. It was not worth it. So as quickly as she had decided that there was some merit to what Mr Brown had said was as quickly as she had dismissed it.

Ms Black considers herself a simple woman, but the food she will be serving tonight is anything but simple.

She has learned the trick of serving a kind of food that gestures towards simplicity and yet isn't. Ms Black hasn't cooked anything herself—her work days are too long—but she has supervised the menu. They will start out with a cream of red peas soup, and in the middle of the table will be a fresh, hot loaf of duck bread that she has sourced from a bakery in Linstead that still does them. The main course will be steamed snapper. She has ordered them to be filleted, but has steamed them in coconut milk and with pimento and okra and Excelsior water crackers. The water crackers is something she insists on. Her guests love these rustic flourishes. Dessert will be a mango sorbet. There will be plenty of wine, and beer, and eventually her guests will retire to her large verandah that overlooks the city of Kingston, and they will talk well into the night—hopefully nothing that gets too heated. Hopefully, nothing about race. This is a dinner party for her neighbours after all. They all live together on this hill—in the top echelons of the island society. Surely race is not part of the texture of their lives.

Just at the point where Ms Black thinks that everything is ready, the intercom rings. It is the security detail posted at her front gate. "Yes, Ms Black. Mrs White and Mr Brown have arrived."

"Wonderful, wonderful!" Ms Black enthuses. "They are the first. Send them in.

3

THE OLD BLACK WOMAN
WHO SAT IN THE CORNER

Virginia Woolf once mused, "I believe that all novels begin with an old lady in the corner opposite," and it makes me think about the old black woman who sat in the virtual corner of my family. I suspect there is a novel to be written about her, and about my family, and about the secrets we kept. It would be a much safer thing to do that—to write a novel with its guise of fiction—rather than this. I think about the old black woman, the way she sat there wrapped in a blanket of silence and secrecy. I did not think about her much as a child, but I think about her now.

"But maybe that's all family is? Just a handful of stories you tell yourself."

I read this line from the manuscript of Branden Jacobs-Jenkins's play, *Appropriate*. It leaves a cold and stinging impression in my heart. I stop as if to gasp, but then the feeling stops, just like that, as suddenly as it had hit me. It is curious. I consider the line again. Why did it hit me, and then why did the impression leave? I think it is almost certainly the truth, but maybe the truth as reflected through a mirror. An inverted truth. So I spin it around in my mind. I spin it until it says something slightly different: *Maybe that's all family is—just the handful of stories we never tell.* And there it is again, the cold shock of truth. I feel the icy bite of it first in my heart, and then it spreads across my entire body.

There are many stories my family did not tell me. They did not tell me about the woman, my father's aunt, who was arrested for murder. It is true that she was not related by blood. She was the wife of my father's uncle, and she had raised cows. So had her neighbours. They raised cows for a living, but a thief in the village was depleting the herds. Every morning they would wake up to find one less cow—either completely gone, or slaughtered and butchered in the field. The police had been informed, but they were useless. Every morning this thing kept on happening. Every morning a congregation of flies would tell them this thing had happened once more—more money down the drain.

Frustrated, the villagers decided to set their own trap. They decided to stay up themselves, hidden in their own fields, until the thief was caught. And so this woman who I had almost never heard about was part of the mob of villagers that caught the thief and part of the mob that beat him to death—slaughtered him just as he had slaughtered the cows.

My family had never intended to tell me this story, but they had gathered—my father, his siblings and their mother— my grandmother—and somehow the edge of the story had slipped out, by a sort of accident. They had tried to usher the story back into the darkness, into the place of cobwebs, but I had grabbed hold of its edge, the trailing hem of it. I had wrenched it back into the light.

The story is told to me almost resentfully, and it goes so far and no more. At this point in time, no one even remembers her name—though she was my father's aunt—my grandmother's sister-in-law. It is only remembered that she murdered a man, and that she went to jail, and that that was the last they ever heard of her. I ask my grandmother again for a name. *Oh*, she says, *who can remember such things now? She was Haitian.* My grandmother says this as if it should explain everything. She was Haitian, which is to say her name was French, and so felt strange in the mouth of a Jamaican so who could bother remembering such sounds—such strange syllables—if one never had to call such a name again. And maybe as well my grandmother was saying she was black and an immigrant, so definitely not worth remembering. It does not matter that my family was a black family. This kind of thing is more common than you might think.

And then my grandmother's eyes light up. She has remembered something—another detail. "Oh yes—she killed my brother, you know. I told you that she was Haitian, yes? Well she made all these bush teas for Massa. It damaged his liver."

They did not want to tell me this story. They did not want to tell me about this woman from Haiti who raised cows and who helped kill a man. And they did not tell me about the old black woman who sat in the corner.

I think about my family—my black family—and the black women we hide from our story.

* * *

Maybe all that a family is, is the stories we do not tell. Maybe all that a family is, is the shape of its silence. For there in that silence lies all the family's shame, and all of its values, and all of its most desperate longings. Often, in the vault of a family's untold stories are the most important things.

I must write this from a peculiar angle. I cannot tell you the stories that were never told to me, or at least that were never told definitively. These are only whispered stories—the little bits overheard when the aunts thought you were not listening, the assorted pieces of a puzzle assembled by you and your cousins as you tried to figure out how things fit together; these are the half stories you swapped at night like little prizes; these are the small snippets told to you by your grandmother when she decided that she was dying and so to hell with it. Perhaps, at the very least, I will change some names—not in order to *make* this fiction, but to acknowledge the fiction that would have already crept in over the years—the guesses, the conjectures. I must acknowledge the incompleteness of it all. I know how to tell stories, but how does one begin to tell silence?

Of course, my grandfather should have been the one to tell this.

Of course, he would not have.

That would be wishful thinking. A stern and proud man, he, perhaps more than anyone else, was the orchestrator of the family's silence. He often liked to say, "I am not a man of words." And this became a family joke. You see, my grand-father was very much a man of words. Words were his live-lihood. I am not the first writer in my family. That was my grandfather. He was a newspaper man, writing and editing for the *New Statesman, Public Opinion,* the *Daily Gleaner.* His best friends were also writers of books and he too had had ambitions of writing his own books one day, though it never happened. He was a man of words. Words had once landed him in jail for sedition.

Perhaps my grandfather really meant that he was not a man of speech, but that would also have been untrue.

My grandmother tells me of the day she sent him, her hus-band, to buy laying chickens for the coop. It was a large family that my grandparents had—eleven children—and so they needed the eggs. My grandmother tells me how, on his way back home he stopped to talk to one of his mentees—a young journalist—and they talked and they talked. My grandmother was waiting, but my grandfather was sitting on a verandah on Slipe Road, talking until the sun was going down. At last, seeing the colours of day change, he gets up to leave. By this time, the chickens in the boot of his car have died. He goes home, wrings his hands, shamefaced. My grandmother laughs when she tells this story—when she tells me about my grand-father whose speech was longer than the lives of chickens.

My grandfather was most definitely a man of words, but he would not have used his words to tell this particular story because to tell it, I suspect he would have had to tell you about another woman that he loved, and maybe then my grandmother would not be laughing at all.

*   *   *

For this, we will call her Miss Henny. It is not her name, but it will do. And in any case, for most of my life I did not know her name. She was just the old woman at Aunt C's house. She had beautiful black skin and impressive white teeth. They were big and straight and I was so young that I did not know that they were false—that they were things that she would take out at night and rest on the bedside table in a cup of water. I knew little about Miss Henny—only that she had been a maid and that even now, in her old age, she still cooked the food at Aunt C's house, and made the beds, and swept the yard. It seemed to me that Aunt C was a generous woman—that she would not dispense of the house-keeper simply because she was old. I saw Miss Henny at least once a year, whenever the family gathered at Aunt C's house. There were so many family gatherings. My grandfather, my grandmother, eleven brothers and sisters, and all of them close, and all of them competing to have the entire family over at their house for one celebration or another. So I saw Miss Henny when the family gathered at Aunt C's, and always I was introduced to her all over again, as all my cousins were. Someone would shout in her ear: "Miss Henny, this is D's son!" or, "This is M's daughter!" And she would smile her big, impressive smile and nod. It strikes me now that the introduction was never returned. She was never introduced to us. As the night wore on she just became a shadow sitting there in her chair, sometimes looking on, sometimes sleeping. She was just the old black woman who sat in the corner. I did not know her story. I did not know her story was connected to my family's—not until the cousins began to whisper: "Do you know who she really is? Do you know her connection to us?"

My grandfather who insisted he was not a man of words instituted the most wordy ritual as part of our annual Christmas dinner. After the feast, and after the family song (yes—my grandfather had composed a family song which we sing with all the gusto of a National Anthem), then it is time for the speeches. The speeches are interminable. Beginning from the eldest child straight down to the youngest, each is expected to stand, give an account of the year just gone and give general Christmas greetings. But of course there are eleven children, and those eleven children have children and grandchildren. So the speeches start with one generation, and then go to the next, and then to the next. My grandfather is long dead, but it seems this tradition will not die. Whenever it is the turn of my youngest cousin to speak we all breathe a sigh of relief because it means there is only one speech left. The last speech belongs to my grandmother. She is the matriarch.

On 25 December 2011, my grandmother stands up at our family dinner to give a kind of speech she has never given before. Her white curls fall over her wrinkled brown face and she leans onto her walking stick. She looks at each of her children gathered before her. She is a mixed woman, my grandmother—Norwegian, Indian, Black—and her children seem to fall, ad hoc, along the full spectrum of her own racial ambiguity. I wonder if it seems odd to her—not that her children have such various racial presentations, but that she has come to an age where they too are old and retired, and with age they have begun to look more alike.

"I've been thinking," my grandmother begins, "that there were things we did in those early days—some decisions that we made—and I know they have caused a lot of hurt. Before I die, we should sit down and talk about these things."

The family erupts.

"OK, Mother Dear. OK." Mother Dear—that is what we call her. They pat her on the shoulder as if she is senile at last. But she isn't and they know it. She is over ninety years old but is more clear-minded than almost any of her children. She has a BlackBerry phone and an iPad. Her husband—my grandfather—had suffered from Alzheimer's and it was a gene he seemed to pass down to his offspring. My grandmother, however, is not so afflicted. She brushes aside these attempts to shush her. They are patronising.

"I'm not losing my head!" she snaps. "I'm old, and these days I'm weak. But I haven't lost my mind. Everything is still up here." And she raises a hand to her head. "And so I've been thinking, while I still have it all up here—while I still remember everything—we should sit down one day so I can tell you why we did the things we did."

Once again the family erupts. Aunt C is on her feet. "All right Mother Dear! All right!" They cannot help themselves. The past is such an uncomfortable place. They have grown so used to the silence. "OK, Mother Dear," they say again. "OK. One day." Which means, never. They never want to talk about these things.

I was not at that family dinner so it is my sister who calls and narrates all of this to me. "Can you imagine it!" she says. "She's ready to talk."

"I know," I say, hardly believing it myself.

I hang up the phone and go online to buy myself a little tape recorder, and soon after that I book my ticket to Jamaica. My grandmother is conscious of her impending death and before she goes she must tell someone about the old black woman who sat in the corner.

The call comes from Jamaica. It is my Aunt C. She is calling my Aunt B who lives in a little town in Europe. But Aunt B is not home. Aunt C must talk instead to Aunt B's husband, Uncle P. It is terrible news. The worst. Aunt C can barely get the words out. "You have to tell B when she comes home that our mother has died." Uncle P almost drops the phone. He is shaking. My grandmother loved to insist that she had no sons or daughters-in-law. They were all her children. She was their mother. And so the news hits my Uncle P as hard as it would have if it had been his own mother. And he does not know how he will tell this news to his wife. He wishes he had been out. He wishes he had not gotten the call. He speaks to Aunt C for just a little longer, both of them with tears in their voices, and then he hangs up and waits for Aunt B to arrive.

She comes home at last and Uncle P is wringing his hands round and round. "B," he says. "B, you must sit down."

Aunt B raises a curious eye but continues towards the kitchen to unpack the groceries she has bought. "B, please!"

he says more sternly. "You must sit down. I have to tell you something."

"What in the world?" she mutters, even as she takes a seat, the panic already rising in her.

Uncle P holds her hand. "B, I am so sorry. I am so very sorry. But Mother Dear has died."

And my Aunt B who had spent the best part of forty years losing her accent—the best part of forty years learning to be classy and European, she suddenly forgets all of this and a guttural wailing sound as if from the most rural village in Jamaica comes up from her chest and out of her mouth. Over and over she screams, "No! No! No! It cannot be!" It does not matter that my grandmother was so old. It does not matter that she had already lived a long, long life. None of it matters. Aunt B is inconsolable. She takes her wig from off her head. She throws it across the room. She beats her chest. "But how, P? How? She wasn't ill. She was OK. She was fine. How? Who told you? How did you find out?"

Uncle P explains it all. "It was C who called while you were out. It was C who told me to give you the news. She said, 'When B comes home, you must tell her that our mother has died.'"

How thick it is, the atmosphere that is grief. And how strange it is when that atmosphere shifts in a second, as if it never was. Aunt B's eyes are suddenly dry, and wide, and curious. "P," she says, a new sternness in her voice, "you must tell me now what C said. You must tell me in exactly the words that she said it to you."

Uncle P is confused. "What? What do you mean?"

"Please P, this is important. You need to tell me exactly what C said."

Uncle P tries to think back to the conversation. What was it that he missed? "I'm not sure B. I just know that C called and she told me, 'When B comes home, you need to tell her that our mother has died.'"

Aunt B sighs heavily and then she almost giggles—a strangely inappropriate school-girl moment of glee. "Oh, thank God!" she says. And then she says it again. And then again. "Oh, thank Heavens." She is out of her seat and walking in a circle. "Oh, thank God," almost crying with relief.

It is a long moment before she is aware of the thoroughly confused face of her husband—her husband of over forty years. She pauses. She sits down again. She realises that there is something she has to tell him—something she has never explained to him. She has never told him about her mother. He has met Miss Henny before. He knows her black skin, and her beautiful big teeth. He knows about the way she sits silently in the corner. She has even made his bed. She has smiled at his children—her grandchildren—but nothing has been explained to him.

I am sitting across from my grandmother; the new tape recorder is in my hands. She knows that I am taping, but still I hide the recorder because I do not want it to feel like a presence between us. She is telling me of the birth of her first child and I glance on the wall behind us, on the picture of my grandmother and grandfather on their wedding day, and I think I have never studied that picture as closely as I should have. I had never before noticed the storm that was behind those smiling faces.

It is a black-and-white photograph. Of course, my grand-parents are much younger people in this, but even in the youthfulness of my grandfather's face, you can see the shape of the old man that he will become. My grandmother is less recognisable—a pretty mulatto girl with large almond eyes seemingly awed by the occasion of her own wedding. Some-times I forget that she is only seventeen in this picture. My grandfather is a decade older. No wonder he has already settled into his features. And I wonder, if I look closely, will I see the shape of the child that was growing inside my grand-mother? The pregnancy had saved her. She would always be grateful for it. Her mother had made plans to pack her things and send her off to America to live with her aunts. A young girl such as she, coming of age, and so many grown men wanting to take advantage. My great-grandmother could not risk it. My grandmother did not want to be sent off. She wanted to live her life, and here, in Jamaica, but without the strict Christian rules of her mother. So it was the pregnancy that saved her—the pregnancy that told her mother, it was too late already. A man had already been there. It was the pregnancy that delivered her from her mother's house and into the arms of her own husband.

Months later, my grandmother gives birth to her first child. His skin is like alabaster; his eyes are hazel-grey; his hair is brown and straight. Stories of the baby and its whiteness spread, and beside those stories, a rumour. Of course the new bride was a mulatto, but her husband was a black man. Not a very dark-skinned black man, but a black man nonetheless —and black and mulatto could hardly produce white! Even the mother by herself could not have produced a white child! A disgrace. The husband had been taken for a fool. It was not his child. It could not be. Surely this was the rightful baby of some American sailor the young wife had messed about with before.

In time the child would become the spitting image of his father—my grandfather. Despite his light skin, strangers would take just one look at him in a crowd and say, "Oh! You must be the boy child of the journalist!" There would be no doubt. But back then, as he lay in his crib, he seemed an impossibility. And so they came. Every day. Visitor upon visitor upon visitor. They said they had come just to pay their respects, but they had come because they had heard the rumours. They had come to behold the white baby.

The days went by and the visitors kept coming. My grand-mother, a teenage mother, confessed that she was tired. On the afternoon when she was dozing off for a nap with the baby in her lap, it irritated her when she heard yet another knock on the gate. She tells me she would have sent the person away if she had not recognised her. It was Henrietta Pin-nock—a woman who sometimes did days'-work for her surly mother-in-law, my grandfather's mother, my great-grandmother. *Aaah*, my grandmother thought. *So that old bitch would like to know if I have really cheated on her son. She has sent this woman to inspect if this is really her grandchild!*

But Henrietta Pinnock was there of her own accord. My grandmother opened the door. "Come in Miss Henny," she said, and let her in. Miss Henny was accompanied by two of her own children—a little girl still sucking her thumb, and a baby still sucking at one of Miss Henny's exposed breasts. Miss Henny introduced them. "This is B," she said, of the little girl at her feet. "And this is C," she said, of the baby on her breast. My grandmother introduced her own first-born, and then for a little while they spoke together as mothers will do. It wasn't long, however, before my grandmother looked at B and C and asked, "So who is their father?" My grandmother insists it was an innocent question. She did not know. She had no idea.

I imagine what must have gone through Miss Henny's own head, how she must have felt something shift in that room— some balance of power. There must have been a part of her that resented my grandmother—this fair-skinned woman who had just upped and married the man who had fathered her own children—that man who had come to her bed again and again and again, but had never mentioned anything about marriage, or the life they could live together as a family. What was it that this woman had that she did not? Colour? Good hair? What was it about this woman that had turned her gallivanting lover suddenly into a family man? But at my grandmother's question, Miss Henny must have realised that this was no woman. She was only a teenager. Miss Henny herself was already in her thirties. She must have felt the full weight and wisdom of her own years. *This naïve little girl*, Miss Henny must have thought, *who knows so little about life and men*.

So Miss Henny told my grandmother the truth. She told it as respectfully as she could. She had not come to cause any ruckus. She had thought my grandmother knew all along. "These are your husband's daughters. We also have two older boys." My grandmother tells me that is how she found out. Her first-born child was her husband's fifth-born.

I listen back to the recording of this conversation and it surprises me that my grandmother had not described the light of a Kingston evening—all its purples and reds and blues—and how it holds within itself a quality of sadness. And yet I see it—the evening and all its colours wrapping itself about my grandmother's shoulders like a shawl. Long after Miss Henny left, she sat outside with the miraculous white baby. She tells me that she cried. And she cried, and she cried. Perhaps she was mourning the little girl that she would never again be.

I realise now that when my grandmother, in her late thirties and early forties, began to gain sons and daughters-in-law and told each one of them that they should do away with titles—told them that she would have nothing to do with "in-laws"—told them that they were simply her sons and daughters, full stop—that this was a habit she had learned before. She had learned that there were other ways of becoming a mother. One did not always need to carry a thing inside for nine months and then give it birth. She insisted that she had no step-children. She told her children that they had no half-sisters or half-brothers. Either this girl is my child or she is not. Either this boy is your brother, or he is not. She allowed nothing in between. I think what an excellent woman she was to have done this. But I also think of what was in between—the things that she would not allow. There was a story there, of course. And a woman.

One need not carry a thing inside for nine months and then give birth in order to be a mother, but I imagine it is a hell of a thing to carry something for nine months, to give birth and to not have that child call you "mother"! I wonder how did Miss Henny, over the years, manage to lose four of her children? Did she lose them the way one loses a five-dollar bill, which is to say, carelessly? Or did she lose them the way so many black women over the years have lost their own children—because of their own poverty, because of all that she could not give them? Did she trade them for a lifetime of anguish and regret? Did she trade them for that same shawl of evening that my grandmother had once wrapped around her own shoulders?

It is true that they were not lost all at once. And not under the same circumstances. After all my grandmother's tears, and after her own mother had failed to console her, saying only, "Well look at that! Look what you done get youself involved in!" my grandmother squared her shoulders. It is what it is. She told her husband, "You have children—well then, I must meet them." And so it was that the little girl that was my Aunt B came to spend a day with her father's wife. When Miss Henny came to collect her, Aunt B started to bawl. It was no regular bawl. The child cried as if she were being killed. My grandmother tried to pry her hands from the door. Miss Henny tried to hold her feet. The neighbours started to open their windows and their doors. What the hell is going on there?! The two women were embarrassed. They decided to wait until the child's father came home. It made no difference. Aunt B kicked and scraped and screamed. She had only come to spend a day with her father's wife—but she would never leave, not until she was a big woman ready to migrate to Europe. My grandmother even had to sign official adoption papers. B became her first daughter.

The two older boys came next. I am not certain that they were even living with Miss Henny at the time. But there was something about them being boys and running rampant, something about them going out of the house with stained collars and dirt under their fingernails, something about them needing the firm disciplining hand of a father, something about them needing the kind of man who would require them to go to church and to recite whole passages of Shakespeare back to him at night. They were boys and they needed a father.

Aunt C continued to live with Miss Henny until she— Miss Henny—got involved with a man who they say was violent. He made things difficult. He would not allow my grandfather to come and visit his own daughter. So C was taken from that household but she would not go to live with her father right away. Instead, she was placed with her father's mother—an old woman who would not see the little girl as her own granddaughter, but rather as the daughter of the woman who did a day's work for her. My great-grandmother saw Aunt C as the servant's child destined to be a servant herself. She was determined to prepare the child for her destiny. My grandmother tells me no details. She says only, "Your great-grandmother was a cruel woman."

One day C arrives at the house where many of her siblings now live—where her father and her father's wife also live. She arrives like a beggar. She has been sent to ask for money from her father but he is not at home. My grandmother is surprised by the fragility of the child, the way she looks constantly over her shoulders, the way she carries herself like a nervous dog that expects to be stoned, and the completely unconscious way in which she often reaches a hand around to her own back as if to feel the shape of something.

"Child," my grandmother says. "Could you take off your shirt?"

C takes off her shirt.

My grandmother observes C's back. She closes her eyes to hide the tears. She swallows. "C, tonight you will sleep here, with us," my grandmother says. And then every night after that.

Thinking about it now, I realise that there would have been many evenings when they were all in the same room—my grandfather and his large family that included my grandmother and her grandchildren, and also Miss Henny and her grandchildren, except that Miss Henny's grandchildren did not know she was their grandmother—did not know to call her Grandma or Nana, or how to sit in her lap and play with her false teeth. I try hard to remember these evenings, to remember some small sign of something that I would not have known how to look for at the time—something which only now I could interpret. I wonder what Miss Henny felt. I wonder what was stored in her heart. She is present, and yet she is the silence of my family. I am drawn to her because of something that vibrates in the space that she has left, even after dying. I suspect she might be the story of my entire island—a story of love and of pain, of men and their mothers, of women who were loved but were never married, of children who were lost and some who were found and some who were beaten because the colour of their skin reminded an old woman of the same skin she wanted to escape, a story of class and race and all its curious intersections.

There she sits—the old black woman in the corner—but no one says a thing. To speak of these things would be to create half-sisters and half-brothers and half-aunts and half-uncles and step-children, and perhaps my family believes that such language would be the end of us as a family. It would be our breaking. So maybe that's all family really is— the handful of stories we dare not tell.

4

THE CRIMES THAT
HAUNT THE BODY

There are crimes that haunt the body, and specific crimes that haunt specific bodies. This haunting is not a memory. It hardly matters if the crime has happened or not—just the fear of it, the knowledge of its possibility causes us to walk the long way home, an extra mile, to avoid the dark corners.

I did not understand this then, when my sister asked me to drop her at the neighbour's house. It was only a street away—barely a ten-minute walk—and so it seemed like sheer laziness that my sister should want me to get into the car and take her. I refused; she called me an asshole; I said she was spoilt, which is strange when I think about it now, me acting as if I was the older sibling. My sister is a few years older but somehow, I had got my license first and so the car and the offering of rides were suddenly within my largesse. But we were never the kind of siblings who fought, so I remember asking—and it was a genuine question—*but why? Why can't you just walk there? I don't understand.* I had become the kind of teenage boy for whom things needed to make sense, things needed to fit into some carefully constructed logic. My sister would not answer the question. She said, *But you're a man. You can't! You cannot understand.*

I remember that fight all these years later because of how much I resented that statement. If my sister's refusal to walk seemed lazy, then this seemed even lazier, this idea that there were things in this world that I could never fully understand because of my body. My sister was telling me a truth I was too young to understand. She could not walk those ten minutes because of a crime that haunted her body in a way that it would never haunt mine.

We lived in a good neighbourhood as neighbourhoods go in Jamaica. The houses were big and gated and the streets were well lit. But there were three empty lots on that road—parcels of land still waiting on their houses. These lots were like tiny forests—a density of trees and vines and grass as tall as fences. Even I held my breath a little whenever I had to walk by these lots at night, wondering what lurked behind the leaves. Whenever there was a crime on the road—a house broken into—we could not help but look at those empty lots and shudder, as if we knew that some evil had escaped from it but had gone back, and that it was still there, observing us, waiting, biding its time.

My sister wanted a ride because we lived in a cul-de-sac. There was no long way round—no extra mile that she could have walked around to avoid the dark corners. She was a young woman. Her friends were young women. They spoke about things—scary things—that some men only know when they read the statistics. My sister understood the likeliness of a particular crime that could be committed on her body. She wanted to make sure such a thing never happened. She knew that the crimes that haunt our bodies do not haunt like ghosts—as something spectral, as something whose only mischief is to rearrange the table. The crime that haunted her body would also have its own body. It would have its own overwhelming smell. Given the chance, it would pull her into the empty lot, into the grass as tall as fences; it would put a hand over her mouth and spread her legs even while she was crying, trying to say *stop. Stop. Please stop.*

There are crimes that haunt the body—specific crimes that our specific bodies are more vulnerable to. I began to understand this when I came off a train in Exeter and a dishevelled man walked up to me. At first, I thought he was a beggar asking for money, but he opened his wallet so I could see the silver flash of a police badge. *I need to ask you some questions.* He was polite. I give thanks for that. He was polite. He apologised that he had to do this, but it just so happened that I fit the description of someone he had been told to look out for—someone coming to Exeter on the London train. And what is that description, I asked him. He looked at his notes as if he needed to. A black man, he said, and closed his book. Only that. A black man. No height, no weight, nothing about hair or eyes or identifying marks. Just a black man. And I turned to look at all the men who were walking right by us then—men with blue eyes and green eyes and grey eyes—men with blond hair and red hair—but all of them comfortably white and therefore unaccused of whatever crime I was supposed guilty of.

I understood the crime that haunts my own body after Liam Neeson's now infamous interview in which he admitted that he wanted to kill me. He wanted to kill a black man after his sister's rape, and any black man would do. He only needed it to be a man, and for the man to be black, maybe stepping off a train from Exeter on his way to give a lecture about the First World War and the epistolary exchanges that it prompted. Neeson says, *I did it for maybe a week, hoping some "black bastard" would come out of a pub and have a go at me about something, you know? So that I could . . . kill him.* And so many people were angry, and so many people were confused that people were angry. And the second group said, *But he didn't actually do anything. He didn't kill a black bastard. And in any case, it was years ago, and he's confessing, and isn't that kind of honesty worth something? Isn't it worth something that he's owning up to it?* I thought they could not know about the crime that haunts my body—a crime that is not spectral, nor hypothetical, because it has happened already. It has happened so many times to bodies like my own, and it can happen again because my body is vulnerable.

I thought about Frank Embree, a nineteen-year-old boy on the train from Mexico and how he was pulled off that train by a mob of a thousand Liam Neesons. I thought about the stories in the papers that described him as a "black brute" and a "negro ravisher". I thought about how they pulled him to the site where they insisted he had raped a fourteen-year-old white girl—Willie Dougherty. I thought about how they made him take off all his clothes so that he could stand before one thousand Liam Neesons, his blackness and his maleness accusing him, and how they gave him 103 lashes, telling him to confess. Confess! Confess! But he would not because he could not. I thought about his ruined skin, torn to pieces as if it were as soft as paper, and the oak tree to which they finally led him, and the rope that was placed around his neck.

And then I thought about Louis Till, the twenty-three-year old American soldier accused of raping a white woman in Italy—Till who had shared a jail cell with Ezra Pound—Ezra Pound, who would immortalise the black soldier in two lines, "Till was hung yesterday / for murder and rape with trimmings". And what about Till's four-year-old son, Emmett, who would only grow to be a fourteen-year-old boy before he became acquainted with the sins of the father, a father he hardly knew but whose blackness and maleness he had inherited. Fourteen years was old enough to make him a black bastard. Fourteen years was old enough that he should be punished for the crime of grabbing and whistling at a white woman. Fourteen years was old enough for him to be dragged out of his great-uncle's house, to have his body mutilated, to have half his head disappeared by a gunshot, and to then have his dead body sunk into a river.

It was only in 2017 that Carolyn Bryant broke the silence she had kept for over sixty years. It turns out she may have exaggerated. Emmett Till had not grabbed her. Emmett Till had not whistled at her. Emmett Till had not made rude sexual remarks to her. But even if he had done those things, would the crime against his body have been justified? I think about that crime, and the men who committed it and who were acquitted of it. I think about the entire life that those murderers lived, and the entire life that Carolyn Bryant lived, and the entire life that was denied a fourteen-year-old boy.

There are crimes that haunt the body, and I wish I had understood that before I broke up with a man whose anger had almost broken me. Though I had tried to end it many times before—to leave—there was something about this moment that made us both know it really was the last time. No apology or promise of therapy was going to change things. He was angry. Predictably so. I thought that was OK because I only needed to survive one last bout of rage then, afterwards, I would be free. But because he knew it was the last time—really the last time—he did not need feel the need to rein in the anger. He could let it become its biggest and most explosive self. This time he could send me eighty-seven texts in one hour, each one nastier than the last. This time he could stand at the top of the stairs and shout down at me, *Oh you just watch! You watch! I can get you deported! You just watch!*

In that moment (I am sorry, but this is true) I thought I would never date a white man again. I would never date someone who, when our love had corroded, could use his whiteness against me as a weapon. I knew that what he said was true—that any story he chose to tell would be believed. It would be believed because of our different bodies, and the different meanings that our bodies produce. Too often the meaning that my black, male body produces is "guilty" and "predator" and "worthy of death".

* * *

I watch the news where William Henry Cosby Jr. is being led to prison and I think, *thank fuck for that!* Three to ten years seems hardly enough for a lifetime drugging and raping women. I watch him being led from the courthouse, a shadow of the affable black father who we allowed into our homes in the 80s. An octogenarian now, he is blind and shuffles with the aid of a stick. This body that has been so broken by age bears no resemblance, for me, to the bodies of Emmett Till or Frank Embree. I am staggered by attempts to place him in that genealogy of unfairly accused black men. I am staggered by the wilful denial of evidence that is so overwhelming.

I can find in my heart no sympathy for Bill Cosby, and yet I can find so much sympathy for the heated conversations sparked by his conviction. I find so much sympathy that it renders me silent. I do not participate in the discussions. I do not intervene. I think I understand both sides, and above the shouting and the protestations and the exasperated sighs, it seems that no one is really talking about Bill Cosby and everyone is talking about their own bodies. My friend, R, has finally had it with a man who has come out in defence of Cosby and whose every word sounds like an apology for rape, who says he is worried about what could befall even him. R says, *You know, it's really not so hard. If you don't want a woman to accuse you of rape, why don't you try this: try not raping women!*

The man recoils at this, and of course I understand why he would do so—why it seems unfair that we should accept responsibility for crimes that our specific bodies did not commit, but that our bodies seem to represent all the same. I know that things are not as simple as R suggests. R knows that things are not as simple as she suggests. We know about Frank Embree. We know about Emmett Till. History tells us that nothing is simple; the present tells us that history has gone nowhere; the present is always tense with the past. I listen to this man fumbling with his words, each one more careless than the last, each one digging a deeper hole. But I do not have better words to offer him and am suddenly overcome by the sadness of this—that our feelings are always so much bigger and more complex than language. Most days we cannot find the words to say precisely the things we would like to say. I listen to him fumbling and wonder if sometimes, like me, he feels himself being led towards an oak tree. I wonder if sometimes, like me, he can almost feel the cool river water closing over his dead body.

In a car in Miami, I am with three black women whose minds I have long been in love with—the driver is a cultural critic, as is the woman sitting beside me in the back. The woman riding shotgun is a poet and essayist whose work has always opened up new spaces in my mind. It occurs to me how safe I feel in the company of their bodies and their intellect, so safe that I can risk asking a question that has been bothering me.

I tell them about the man in Jamaica who, until the day before, was on the run from the police. The charge was rape, and one of the most brutal I had heard. He worked at a hotel and had secured the job despite a criminal record. He hadn't worked there for a week when they say he went into a room and held two female guests at gunpoint. He raped one while pointing the gun at the other, and then had them switch places. At some point the gun fell from his hand; one of the women grabbed the weapon, shot the man, and he ran away, escaping over the balcony, a trail of blood behind him.

My god! The three women breathe. And, *Wow!*

But they caught him yesterday, I tell the women, *and the story he tells is so different.*

This is the story the man tells: there was no gun. Well, not at first. It was just his first week on the job, but already he knew of the seedy side of the hotel industry and that it could be lucrative. He knew that sometimes guests would ask more from him than just room service. He says the women had invited him to the room. They wanted a threesome. He obliged and that's what he was doing. He said there was no gun—not until the door opened suddenly and it was the husband of one of the women. It was the husband who drew the gun; it was the husband who shot him and he had to escape over the balcony. He never stopped running, he said. He was so afraid. And it was only later that he heard his name on the news and he heard this whole story about a rape at gunpoint.

But, says M—the essayist—and then pauses. *But,* and she pauses again. *But that makes so much more sense!*

Yes, I say. *I know.* But the knowing brings me no comfort. I know why it is important to believe accusations of rape. I understand why we must believe the testimonies of women, so I do not know what to do morally with these moments of doubt, these moments when my belief does not come easily. There is a wonderfully vulnerable prayer in the Gospel of Mark, as doubtful as it is faithful. *I believe, Master,* says the father of a possessed child. And then, *Help my unbelief!*

I know, says M from the front seat of the car, as if to echo my own words. And then over and over, *I know, I know, I know*—both shaking and nodding her head. *I know. You see, it's not that we believe women. It's that we believe whiteness.*

And there was a sudden moment of comfort for me in that car. I realised how silly it was to worry that sometimes my convictions and my politics are not simple or straight-forward—that in fact they are messy and conflicted. It is OK to hold onto a principle, even while being aware of its exceptions. In this world that we live in now, I understand the importance of belief, especially if it is all that one can offer. But if you tell me that belief must extend to everyone without exception, and that it is also retroactive, that my belief must extend to Carolyn Bryant and Willie Dougherty, then it cannot; it will not. If I believe in their testimonies then I become one of the men who pulled Emmett from his great-uncle's house, and one of the men who pulled Frank from the train. But I cannot kill those boys all over again. I cannot participate in the crime that haunts my body.

It took thirteen years for my friend, T, to stand in front of one of those squat, ugly buildings that passes for a police station in Jamaica, the dullness and unfriendliness of its architecture only surpassed by the dullness and unfriendliness of the officers who work inside. Thirteen years after she had been pulled into the grass as tall as fences; thirteen years after a man she knew, a man she had called "uncle", parted her fourteen-year-old legs; thirteen years after every thrust made her face scrape against a guava tree.

Inside, a female corporal leads her to a bathroom without a door and tells her to take off her clothes. The corporal has to confirm that T really does have a vagina. According to Jamaican law, "rape" is the insertion of a penis into a vagina; only vaginas are rape-able, so she must confirm that the alleger of a rape is in fact someone capable of being raped. Satisfied by T's vagina—that she has one—the corporal instructs her to keep her clothes off for a while longer because now they must administer the rape kit and swab for evidence.

But it was thirteen years ago, says T.

Yes, ma'am. But is procedure. We have to do it, says the officer in that way that will brook no argument.

A half-hour later, with her clothes back on, T is standing in front of the officer who is leafing through one of those big ledger books that are the hallmarks of these stations. Sometimes, behind the counter, you can see mountains of them piled up to the ceiling. It is where reported crimes are written down and where I often think they go to die, shut away forever in those books. Having finally arrived at a clean page, the officer is ready to make an incident report in the ledger book. *Yes, ma'am. So when did this incident occur?*

T sighs. *It was thirteen years ago.*

Thirteen years, ma'am! And the officer raises her brows as if she is hearing it for the first time. *That is a long time!*

T says there was a part of every moment of the two hours spent in that station that she was ready to leave—ready to just walk away. It was only that she had prepared herself for all of it, even though she knew the statistics and knew it was unlikely that anything would come of it. But there was no moment she was more ready to leave than when the officer said incredulously, *Thirteen years, ma'am!*

It is possible that at that very moment, in another country perhaps, a man has come forward after ten years, or twenty, or thirty, to finally tell his story. Despite having lived a whole life, and having had a career and a family—he has come forward now to tell the story of the gym teacher or the priest, and not a solitary soul will raise their eyes and say, *thirty years! It took you a whole thirty years to come forward?* Empathy and understanding will be offered immediately. He will be believed immediately. Implicitly, everyone will know why it took thirty years. They will know the powerlessness and fear he must have felt as a child and the memories that must have haunted his body all these years. They would understand the bravery of this moment, what it means for him to come forward with his story—at last—and they will hold his hands and his shoulders and say, *Good for you! Good for you!*

I know there is a crime that haunts the bodies of black men, and a crime that haunts the bodies of women, and I know that these hauntings are not equal. I know that women have wept over the slaughtered bodies of black men— sometimes their fathers or their brothers or their sons or their husbands. I know they have marched and signed petitions and stood in front of parliaments and screamed, and sometimes they just wish that men would weep for the bodies of their women in the same way—would march and sign petitions and stand in front of parliaments and scream.

There are crimes that haunt the body, and I wish I understood it back then, because I would not have asked my sister any questions. I would have jumped in the car immediately and taken her anywhere that she wanted to go. And though I think she knows that I would drive a thousand miles for her, sometimes the greater love is the one that is willing to drive just a few metres—just from one gate to the next—any distance, no matter how small, just to make certain, as she was trying to make certain, that the crime that haunted her body would never become flesh.

5

AN ABSENCE OF POETS
AND POODLES

This is what happened: somewhere in northern England I entered a house after a long train ride. It was a grand house marked by a kind of gentility. It sat in a gentle landscape; gentle walks into the countryside rolled out from its centre, and one imagined that in times gone by gentlemen in top hats would come knocking on the door. It was the kind of house that sits stoically in the present but aches towards its past.

In the house, a small dog runs up to me, wagging its tail and licking my ankles. The owner of the house, who has just picked me up from the train station and is helping me with my bags, calls to the dog.

"Lola! Lola, stop!"

"Her name is Lola?" I ask, incredulously, and stoop down to pat Lola's black curls. Lola turns on her back to offer me her tummy.

"Yes. We named her Lola."

"That's uncanny," I say. "My friend in Jamaica has a dog—a poodle-Shih Tzu mix exactly like this, and her name is Lola as well."

It is now my host's turn to look at me incredulously. He opens his mouth, "Oh my! I didn't realise you had dogs in Jamaica!"

My brows furrow and my host is suddenly embarrassed. He stammers but then says nothing. The small silence is awkward between us. In that moment, I am certain I know what it is he meant to say. He meant to say, "I didn't realise you had HOUSE dogs in Jamaica." Or else, "I didn't realise you had houses in Jamaica—the kind of houses that could accommodate house dogs. This is not my imagination of Jamaica." But he didn't say this, which was probably for the best, and even then I could see that inside his own mind he was having his own small battle and adjusting his thoughts.

"Shall I show you to your room?" he asks me next. "You can relax a little before the reading tonight."

Somewhere in northern England I entered a house a second time for the day. It had been a long day of train rides and car rides and in the evening, a poetry reading. In the morning I would have to catch the early train and return home, but tonight—tonight I will rest. Lola does not run up to greet me this time. She is sleeping in her basket. The owner of the house kneels down to pet her and she whimpers blissfully kicking out a leg and turning in her sleep.

"Would you like a nightcap?" he offers. He has been oddly silent for the car ride back home and so his voice almost takes me by surprise.

"Thank you. I would like that."

I go to my room to put down the books I had read from and then join my host in the sitting room. There is a glass of sherry waiting for me—and it is this, the sherry, the fireplace, the mantelpiece (not Lola)—that all seems to belong to that world of gentility that the outside suggests.

The silence feels awkward again but only because looking to my host I see that he is on the verge of saying something, but is struggling with the words. His brows are furrowed and every now and again his mouth parts to speak, but then he closes it again.

"That was an extraordinary reading you gave," he says, at last.

I smile. "Thank you."

"No, no, no," he says, almost impatiently, as if I haven't quite understood what he is saying. "It really was quite extraordinary. One of the best readings I've heard."

He is almost trembling now and I'm stunned by the tenor of his praise. It feels that a mere "Thank you" will not do.

He turns then to look at me and I see now the confusion on his face. "What was it like," he asks, "having a talent like that and growing up in a place like Jamaica?"

Yes, I leave a space in this essay for the silence I have been trying to write about—that silence in which so many things that should be said are never said. In that moment I could not say the things I wanted to say, nor ask the questions I would have liked to ask, because I would have appeared rude. I would have seemed like an inhospitable guest. And also, I could not say them because they were too important. I looked into the man's eyes—wide and earnest—and in the blue of those eyes, the grey-blue of his questions, I also saw the blue of the Caribbean. In the blue of the Caribbean, I saw the green of my island, its shape like a giant manatee swimming out to deeper sea. I saw the whole Caribbean, the islands so quaint; on those islands was an absence of poets and poodles, which is to say, they were primitive places.

In his eyes there were no poodles, but there were, in fact, many dogs. I could see them clearly, marauding around rubbish heaps. Malnourished dogs—mongrels mostly—whose ribcages protrude like xylophones, like some as yet unplayed music. I thought, maybe these are the dogs about which, on 5 February 2007, a sleep-deprived German ambassador to Jamaica wrote a public letter. Whether this letter was *about* the dogs or addressed *to* the dogs, I am still not certain. His Excellency complained that the mutts barked with such gusto and so incessantly that for six months he hadn't had a full night's sleep. He even quoted the Noise Abatement Act. He asked respectfully that the Noise Abatement Act be quoted to the dogs. He asked that they be made aware that, dogs though they may be, they were in fact breaking the law. He respectfully requested, that across the island dogs were to be quiet between 10 p.m. and 6 a.m., to allow foreign diplomats uninterrupted sleep. An absence of poodles, but an island full of uncouth, unmannered, uncaring bitches and sons of bitches—that's what the Caribbean was. That is what I saw in the man's eyes.

And in his eyes there were no poets to speak of—no one sitting at their desk, a library of books rising behind them, writing, considering carefully the place of each word. There were storytellers though: old, toothless women who would quote the Bible and who would read omens in the moon and who would tell such charming stories to a circle of barefoot grandchildren in tattered clothes—stories about Bredda Cow and Bredda Rat. It is not that this man did not know that Derek Walcott was also from the Caribbean, or Kamau Brathwaite, or Lorna Goodison—but that these facts lived in such separate and isolated rooms. They never met each other in the long corridor of his brain—that corridor being so thick with carpet that guests walked by each other's rooms, but softly. No one is ever disturbed. No one meets each other in the mornings at the breakfast table.

I never do get around to answering his question. It is just left there, awkward and lingering in the air. I have my own questions and though they are un-asked, they too seem to hang in the air like a gnarled fruit. I would like to know why I seem to him to be such an unlikely product of my country. I would like him to tell me if he sees all black intellectuals—artists, poets, composers, scholars, novelists— as unlikely products of their communities. I would like him to tell me if he thinks accomplishment is a peculiar outcome of the black experience? And also, I would like him to tell me what precisely he had meant by "a talent *like that*"? What was my talent like? What was its shape, its sound? Did it have eyes, or fur, or legs? Could he tell me what kind of poet he had expected me to be? Was there a specific role I had not fulfilled? And had I been the kind of poet he had expected of me, would that not have prompted a whole other set of questions? Would I have been writing a whole other essay?

It was late and so I went up to my room. It was a grand room in a grand house, but the questions that prevented me from falling asleep immediately seemed suddenly grander than them all, heavier than stone or bricks. I opened the large bay window and lit a cigarette. It had been a day full of journeys and I was tired, but looking out just then at the fields outside and the walking paths that rolled out from the house, they seemed so much less gentle than they had earlier, as if all that gentility hid a world of danger.

6

THE BOYS AT THE HARBOUR

In Kingston, at night, the harbour is beautiful—almost as beautiful as the boys who gather around it, the boys who are still young and still have dreams as big and bright as the fireworks that light up the waterfront each New Year. On that night—the first day of the year—the waterfront does not belong to the boys, but to a new throng of people who wouldn't normally venture into this part of town, people who have learned a long time ago how not to see these boys. And maybe even tonight, though it isn't the New Year, if you pass by the harbour, you will not see them either, sitting as they do in the shadows, under the sweet almond trees—these boys talking about their big and bright dreams.

It hurts a little to hear them speak these dreams—to hear them speak about a future I sometimes doubt will be theirs. *Me going to live in one of dem big, big house pon de hilltop,* the boy says, looking behind, not to the water but to the hills that rise over this brutal city. I follow his gaze and look to those lights, glittering like sequins on the hills—the hills to which the New Year's crowd will return. The house that I grew up in is on those hills as well, and I too will return there in just a couple of hours. My father's house is emitting one of those lights. *And me not going to work fi nobody neither,* the boy continues. *Me going to be mi own boss. Just a little money fi start mi business. That's all me need.* He says none of this as if it is a question—as if the future is in any doubt. He says it as a simple fact—something that will happen in the near future. *When me start mi own business, you will see where it take me!* And he looks again to the hills.

I try to smile, but I worry that my smile might not be convincing, or that the boys might think it patronising. I wonder when it was that I stopped believing in the world as they do. It strikes me as selfish, my lack of faith. If anyone should have lost faith, it is these boys who have been kicked out of their houses, who have slept in gullies, or in bus sheds, or right here at the harbour. I wonder how it is that they have kept their faith, but maybe faith is all the more important when you have so little else.

There is a sound, strange and terrifying, like the strangled voice I imagine death might speak with.

Kling-Kling! Saville says, pointing, and we all look towards the harbour, to the thing he is pointing at, and I only barely see the shape of a bird sailing across the water—a bird that is the same colour as the night, so it is quickly lost within it. Soon there is only its sound. I think about the bird, about its feathers that just became one with the water. I think of the water as a large feathered thing—a giant crow sulking in the night.

The boys will stay here, talking, laughing, arguing until the sky turns pink and the sun begins to rise up over the harbour, its light shimmering off the zinc roofs and fences of the shanty town nearby—and at that time the harbour will not be as beautiful as it is now. But there are many hours to kill until then. Sometimes, in the wee hours of the morning, a car, its tinted windows wound all the way up, will creep by. It will not stop. Not at first. It will drive right by the group of boys and then turn right, driving up past the National Gallery, and then it will be lost to the hapless streets, gone out of sight. In a minute or two it will return from the other side. Here it comes again—creeping by the waterfront. One of the boys might then ask, "Who working tonight?" and someone will shrug and walk towards the road, towards the car making its second approach. I notice there is always something a little exaggerated in the swing of the boy's hips as he walks out. Maybe the car will stop this time, and the boy will lean into the window that has finally come down. I imagine words are exchanged. I have never been close enough to hear the words, but the boy might come back after to gather his things and then will go back and into the car.

Or else it happens like this—the car does not stop on its second approach. I imagine the driver sees the boy approaching and then suddenly puts his foot on the gas. The car speeds away. It will not come back a third time. It has gone back up into those hills, the driver suddenly afraid of his own desires.

You see, British, O'Neil says, about one of these disappearing cars, *Kingston naah work like how it did work one time. One time gone you fuck a man and you get a little $5,000. But things mash up now. These days, man fraid say him a go get rob,*

*or him a go get scam, or him a go get stab up. Is pure free fuck
a run it now in Kingston. Things mash up.*

In the beginning, I had not told them that I lived in Britain. I had hardly said anything about myself, though it seemed I never needed to. They were observant, picking up on clues I didn't know I was dropping. They could see things—even the shape of a black bird against the harbour. I always wondered about their easy acceptance of me, an acceptance that would never ask for money or help of any kind. It was enough for me to arrive with a bottle of rum, ice, a bottle of Ting to chase the liquor. It was enough to just sit by the harbour and talk.

You know battyman in Jamaica? Saville once asked. And I said, *Yes, of course.* He then went through his list—trying to find our six degrees of separation—or just the one degree; Jamaica wasn't so big after all. But for every name he called, I had to shake my head. *No. No, I'm sorry. I don't know that person.* Jamaica wasn't big, but there were so many different Jamaicas that it was possible to live in worlds that really had never intersected. He seemed disappointed. I thought about it for a while. *Dexter*, I finally offered. *I knew Dexter.*

Dexter who had once lived here—not outside on the harbour, but in the Ocean Towers above, a middle-class enclave that was still downtown. Dexter, who had taken me to my first gay party up in the hills. Dexter, one of Jamaica's most talented fashion designers. Dexter, still so young and who had died just two months ago—apparently stabbed to death by a man he had only just bailed out of jail. Dexter, whose face had been in all the newspapers recently.

Yeah man! Of course me did know Dexter. And then he looked at me with a new understanding. *Oooohhhh! You come from that side of Jamaica.* It wasn't an accusation, just an understanding. An acknowledgement.

One night it is a police car, its blue and red lights flashing, that slowly drives along the waterfront. I am sitting by my own car, talking to the boys. The police car stops. We are all suddenly afraid.

What oonoo doing out here at this time? the officer barks.

We're just chatting, I answer.

Chatting time done. Time for you to move on, the officer says. He looks at me, and looks at the boys, and he shakes his head. He doesn't try to hide his disapproval.

I go into the driver's seat and a few of the boys pile in. We drive away.

Is because you is a car man why dem stop, O'Neil explains. *Usually dem don't trouble we. We is walk-foot bwoy. But you is a car man. Dem trying to protect you, British.*

For a while we drive in no real direction, along Marcus Garvey Drive and towards the port. For all its reputation, Kingston is a city that definitely sleeps. It is almost surprising how empty the streets are, how desolate it can be—the street-lights and the moon, illuminating the dismal factories, the rust of it all. Soon we are on the causeway and its familiar smell of dead fish enters the car. If we continue we will have to pay the toll and drive into the maze of Portmore. We circle back, back to the harbour. This time I park my car in a less conspicuous place, but the police have set my mind wondering about the night and all the dangers inside it. Out here, on the harbour, we are only a stone's throw away from some of Kingston's most dangerous ghettos. I think of these ghettos in Conradian terms—as a dark and brooding place—a place where a restless evil stirs. A recent study tells me that the murder rate in this part of the city is even higher than the death rate in Iraq during the height of war. I wish I did not think of my own country in these terms—a heart of darkness. But I do.

Is it usually safe out here? I mean, safe for you?

They shrug. *Safe enough.*

The police don't bother you?

Well, yeah. Maybe if dem see you walking pon de road at night and dem think that maybe you is a badman or something like that. But you see, and the boy is smiling, *when dem hold you, you just tell dem de truth one time. Yes. That's what you need to do. You look dem straight in the eye and say, OFFICER! Yu nuh see seh me a battyman? Me naah trouble nobody! Me not no murderer! Me a battyman!* He performs all of this for me. Wriggling out of the hands of the officer, making this brave declaration. It is an extravagant performance. He laughs. *And you see, when you say that now, well . . . dem will let you go. Dem don't want to hold onto you after that. And you see, this is Jamaica. Nobody not going to claim say dem is a battyman if dem is not really a battyman.*

I laugh with the boys, but I think about this identity that has left so many of them homeless on the streets, and yet protects them. This identity that they no longer run away from—that on some nights can become their sword and shield.

Well, what bout de badman? I ask, pointing with my lips towards the nearby ghettos.

No. Nuh really. Dem know seh we a battyman too. Everybody know. But dem don't usually trouble we. You haffi be careful still, but . . .

He never finishes the sentence, and I know that there are dangers the boys will not tell me about. Not yet. I think of a line from Dionne Brand. *If I am peaceful in this discomfort, is not peace, / is getting used to harm.* I think of the ways that our bodies might grow used to harm. And maybe my question could not be answered after all because the answer could only be felt in the body. A friend once tried to describe this to me—the precarity that is Jamaican street life: *Sometimes you and your crew out on the corner, just chilling, and then you just feel a thing. Like maybe a change in the wind or a kind of quiet. Everybody feel it the same time. Everybody know how to feel it. You and your crew don't ask any question. You just move. Immediately. And sometimes is nothing at all, but plenty times is something—and if you don't learn how to move just like that, just because you have a feeling, well* . . . *that's when you dead.*

This month I have found the boys at the harbour, but in another month they will leave just because of a feeling, or a change in the air. Then at a later time they will return. They are always moving. There are always turf wars. Always conflicts. And sometimes they do not move fast enough. Sometimes there are deaths. I have seen the boys empty their pockets. I have seen the glint of knives and pickaxes—these things they always carry for their protection but that don't always work.

Remember dem days in New Kingston, Saville begins, *when Judgement did always come down pon we. Long time now we don't see Judgement.*

And they are all smiling, as if this memory is sweet.

Judgement? I ask.

Yes. Is dat we did call it. Judgement. Sometimes a carload o" man would drive up. Man who come to beat we up. Dem come out wid stone and bat, and dem times now we have on we dress and we make-up and we high heels. We look like real woman. We working. But every now and then a carload o" man come to beat we up. To beat up all the battyman, and we haffi run fi cover. We running in we high heels. Everybody bawling out, JUDGEMENT!

And now they are laughing—laughing so hard that they are clutching their sides, this memory of themselves scampering away like gully rats.

It was Jermaine who did teach we how to stand up fi weself, one says, and everyone suddenly catches their breath; something solemn has entered.

God rest his soul. Jermaine.

I do not ask—at least not on that night—how it was that Jermaine died. In time I have learned this is not unusual—this roll call of friends who have died. Omar. Mark. Colin. Jermaine. Dexter.

What did Jermaine teach you?

One day him just say him wasn't going to run any more. Probably him did just tired of it. Him say why we should run when we more than them. Him say him not going to make one more straight man beat him up. And is so we start to stand up fi weself and fight.

I have a sense of this moment. This moment when the homeless boys of New Kingston suddenly entered Jamaica's consciousness. And it was this that did it—their sudden refusal to be cowed or bullied. Their insistence on standing up proud in their high heels and their wigs and their tight dresses. It frightened the men who were really just cowards, who had come just to have a little bit of fun, just to rough up the sissy boys a little, as if to prove their own masculinity, and who came back instead with all the bruises, all the cuts on their own skins. Beaten up by battymen! This wasn't the script they had come to know. They did not know beautiful gay boys could stand up for themselves. They did not know beautiful gay boys could fight back.

Suddenly, the boys were in the newspapers. They had been given a new name. The Gully Queens. The residents of New Kingston complained about them. These boys were squatters, prostitutes, thieves, murderers. They beat up innocent people. They were the worst of the worst. Why weren't the police doing something?

Put your ear close to the waves of the Kingston Harbour on a night when the city is sleeping, and you might hear so many stories—the words soft and fluttering against the dark feathers of the water—stories about the cars that they have climbed into, the big men that they have met—business leaders, politicians, dancehall artistes who some nights put their mouths against the mouths of these boys, kiss them so deeply, but then use those same mouths to sing terrible songs about them. You will hear stories about the magnificent houses they sleep in just for a night, and stories about how, on another night, they will have to sleep under the stars. Put your ear close to the waves and you might learn, in case you ever need to know, how to stay clean and tidy even without an abundance of fresh water, how to wash the body with pods of ackee and deodorise your underarms with lime, how to press your clothes between pieces of cardboard so that when it is morning, you can walk throughout the city feeling proud, smelling good, your head held high.

Cleanliness—it is important to the boys. The money that they earn, they spend on their cleanness, and the need to be unblemished. When they argue amongst themselves, it is the easy insult that they draw for. *Look how your skin spotty, spotty!* And the insulted boy will lift his shirt at once, will step out into the street and walk as if on a catwalk. *No, mi love! Look! Look! Mi skin clean and pretty! Clean like dunce pickney school-book! Not a spot, mi love!*

Tonight, however, they tell me stories about families. Stories about how to lose a family, or how a family might lose you. And stories about how you might gain a new family, about "sisterhood", which is what the boys say exists between them.

Mi madda never kick me out, says Dale. *She never want me to go. She cry when me did leave. But the people in the community—dem did start harass we. Dem seh me did trouble a little boy. It wasn't true. But dem woulda do something to mi family—to mi madda—so me leave.*

Saville's story is different. *One day when mi madda and fada find out bout me, mi fada take a plate, and a cup, and a knife and a fork and him tell me this is your plate, and your cup, and your knife and your fork. And him mark dem and tell me dem is the only ones me should use, because him wasn't going to eat out of the same plate or drink out of the same cup as any battyman. And we live like that for a few months until is like him couldn't take it any more, and him tell me to leave. Me did have a job at first. Me get a room in St Thomas, but when me lose the work, me couldn't pay the rent and dat's how me did end up pon the road fi a year.*

He doesn't live on the road any more, and many of the boys here do not. Homelessness is a state they fall in and out of. But when it is night, they come back here to see each other, to see their family. They are sisters.

I usually drive Saville back to the room that he rents on my way home. On the drive he leans his head against my shoulder and his hand is on my knee. *I like you,* he says. *You're really funny. And you listen.*

I concentrate on the road hoping that he doesn't feel the sudden tension in my own body.

I don't live here, I remind him. *I'm going back soon.*

He shrugs.

And you're twenty-four, I say, trying another tactic. *I'm thirty-nine.*

And now he's sitting back up. *So what!?* It is sharp, almost angry. *Dat is no difference at all! My first boyfriend was your age and dem times I was only thirteen! I only like men older than me.*

With the streets so empty, it doesn't take very long for us to get to the community where he now lives, but he doesn't get out of the car. I turn off the engine and he tells me about this man that he was once in love with.

It take me a whole year to get over dat one. I did love him.

But you were only thirteen! He could have been your father.

That's what I think, but I do not say it. My throat feels tight. I do not feel I have the right to tell him that he was abused, but a strange rage is building in me. Instead, I ask, *How long did it last?*

Three years, he tells me. *Till I was sixteen. Well, almost sixteen.*

And why did it end?

Saville shrugs. He looks out the window. *Me did get too old for him. Him did want somebody younger.*

And that was your first sexual relationship?

Oh no! Saville says, and he's almost laughing. *No man, not at all. The first one was horrible. I was . . . and then his voice dips . . . I was molested. From I was three to bout ten years old.*

And the answer that I already know surprises even me.

Your father?

Yes, mi fada.

And I think about this father—this father who separated plates and cups and forks and knives—who told his son he wasn't going to eat from the same plate as no battyman—this father who kicked him out into the streets is the same father who molested him for years. And the thing that was in my throat, the thing that was anger, has now dissolved into something else, into a bubble of things I think I cannot say. I reach across and hold his hand.

The boys enlist my help in carrying out a robbery, though I know nothing about it or the help that I offered until days after the fact. They have added me as friends on Facebook and so O'Neil knows that I am near Montego Bay. He calls me on WhatsApp. *Mi see you deya country, British.* Montego Bay is in fact Jamaica's second city, but to the chagrin of Montegonians, people from Kingston still refer to it as "country". There is "town" and there is "country", and only Kingston is "town". *Yeah, I'm in Mobay*, I confirm.

And when you a guh back?

Tomorrow.

Mi can get a ride? Me and mi bredrin. We down dis side too.

I agree to give them a ride back and say that I'Ll be in touch the next day.

I am not actually in the city of Montego Bay but in a village ten miles or so outside it. I do this pilgrimage on all my trips to Jamaica, spending time with a woman I love, the poet Jean Binta Breeze, chatting on her verandah and looking out to the sea on the other side of the road. The water here is different from Kingston Harbour's—cleaner, and yet smelling even more strongly of salt and sea and fish. Poor health has made it difficult for Jean to travel. Sometimes, even going from her verandah across the road to put her feet in the sea takes a lot out of her. So I go to her, and there is no schedule in the time we spend together.

The next morning there are missed calls on my phone. O'Neil wants to know when I will be heading back to Kingston. It annoys me. I call back to say, I can't give a time.

But what you doing?

I want to say, *I am here to sit on a verandah. I am here to smell the sea and the salt and the fish and just to be with a friend. I'm not on your schedule.* What I end up saying is, *Look—I will call you when I'm ready.*

Two hours later and the phone is ringing again. O'Neil says he and his friend have been up since 4 a.m., when they were forced to leave the house they had been staying at. He says nothing else about this, only that they are tired and hungry. That they have no money. So please—when will I be heading back to Kingston?

I almost snap. *Look, I said I will call you when I am ready!*

In the early afternoon I drive back towards Montego Bay. The phone is ringing again but now I do not answer. I decide to call when I'm in the city. O'Neil resorts to texting—each text more anxious and frustrated.

At last I turn into KFC where we have agreed to meet. He and his friend walk sulkily towards the car. They put their belongings in the trunk before getting in. O'Neil mutters a greeting and then pushes the seat all the way back as if to go to sleep. His friend stretches across the back seat. I try to remind myself that these really are just boys. Sometimes they are immature. Sometimes they throw tantrums which can seem to make little sense.

And they are so small, I realise, that the cramped car seats are sufficient beds for their bodies. They sleep. I drive through the army checkpoint as Montego Bay is under a State of Emergency. The soldiers wave me on and I drive towards Kingston. Back in town, the boys are awake and in a seemingly better mood. I drop them off and they wave goodbye brightly, but I am probably the one more annoyed at this point.

Two days later I see a picture of O'Neil and his friend being circulated on Facebook. The word "WANTED" is in all caps above the picture. The post reads, "Does anyone know these two thieves? They stayed with my friend in Montego Bay and when he went to work at 4 a.m. they stole everything from his house, laptops and phones. The police have been contacted."

I decide then that I will not return to the harbour.

I do not go back to the harbour but I still think about it, how sometimes the quiet of the night is disturbed by a rumbling in the sky, lights flashing between the clouds—a plane coming in to land at Norman Manley International Airport.

One night Saville looked at the dark bird descending, a sort of pain written across his face. *Just one more month,* he said to no one in particular. *One more month then that is me.*

You leaving? I asked.

Yeah. Me a go to Argentina.

Argentina? Entiende español?

Sí. He said, his eyes still on the landing plane. *Tengo un amigo en Buenos Aires. Vamos a abrir una tienda.*

His Spanish had quickly exceeded my own. I switch back to English. *Where did you learn Spanish?*

He didn't have time to answer before another boy decided to show off his own language skills. He spoke haltering snippets of a language I did not immediately recognise. *German?* I asked.

Dutch, he told me.

Amsterdam. Argentina. These are the places that they dream about. They would rather stay here. They would rather build their own houses on the hills. But if it gets too much, and if they ever decide to leave this island, they explain that it is now so hard to get asylum in English-speaking countries —in England or in Canada or in the US. So they dream about a world bigger than the world I dreamed about when I was their age. They dream about languages I never cared to learn. On Facebook they make friends with men from all around the world—older men—men that one day, in some future, they might meet at an airport, and if such a thing should happen they would like to say to him, in his own language, *Hello. Thank you for meeting me here.*

In Kingston, at night, the harbour is beautiful. It is almost as beautiful as the boys who gather around it, or maybe it is the boys who make the harbour beautiful—the boys who sit and watch the planes coming in—the planes that are as big and as wonderful as their dreams, their dreams that I have come to share, and hope for, and pray for—these complicated boys in whom you could so easily lose faith, unless you decide, like them, to hold onto it.

7

THE BUCK, THE BACCHANAL,
AND AGAIN, THE BODY

I t was two weeks after Carnival was done and dusted away
that the buck appeared. And I think that was bad manners
or at least bad timing, but maybe good timing and manners
is not something to be expected of ghoulish beings, especially
bucks. In any case Carnival was done and people say life had
already come back to normal. Everything had come back,
including the pious Christians who had gone to Tobago to
hide out. Including Trinidad itself that had gone wherever it
is that entire countries go to, 'cause sometimes it could feel
like that, like the island itself had just packed up and gone
along with the Christians, and along with good behaviour,
gone off somewhere to hunker down and keep safe during
the Carnival week.

Some people say that Carnival is its own country and that
Carnival have its own citizens, and that those citizens (like
me) are not always from Trinidad, and that those citizens
(unlike me) are not always human or corporeal. There is a
feeling in the country called Carnival that a new kind of
space exists, and the space is a generous one. It can accommodate all manner of things—not just the bad behaviour

and the wutlessness and the wining—but also jumbies, and the ancestors, and Shango.

On J'Ouvert morning it might happen like this: you walking in that cool before-day-morning, and the Laventille Rhythm Section playing a kind of music that feel like a haunting—a kind of music that waking up not just the few people who stupid enough to be inside their houses trying to catch sleep at this time—but something older and deeper. Just like that a feeling might pass through you, something that make the hairs on the back of your neck stand up. You don't know how to name this feeling but you know that other people feeling it too. A woman who is just in front of you, marching with a fire held in front of her, the black smoke from her home-made torch lost into the night air—you notice how she shiver like a sudden shock of electricity has passed through her. She break away from the crowd and march in a wide circle as if to claim a space on that road. And people not stupid. They know to give her the space that she is claiming. She have a Pepsi bottle full up of kerosene in her pocket. She turn it to her mouth. Then she hold the fire in front her mouth and breathe out a spectacular breath of flames. *Watch the dragon,* you think to yourself. *Watch the dragon dance.* You feel the heat of the fire all over you skin, and then another woman who standing beside you is just nodding. Her eyes closed tight but she nodding just like those women you grow up with in church—that kind of nod when the preaching sweet—that nod that come right before the Amen! The woman beside you nodding in that way—nodding at this just-wake-up feeling that you don't have a name for. And then she name it. Such a soft word on her lips, and her eyes still closed. But she say the word, "Spirit!" And you look out on the crowd again and realise is more than just a crowd of people, but also a crowd of spirits. The thought might even come to you how strange it is that the feeling of being out of body is always felt inside the body.

On a morning such as this, it won't even matter to you that as the Laventille Rhythm Section playing their music, and as the woman is breathing her fire, that there is another set of people who looking like they just come down from North America, and their mouths open wide, wide, wide like they catching flies, and they shouting to each other, "Ohhh my gaawwwdd! Isn't that, like, amaaazing!" and they taking pictures of the woman breathing fire—it won't really matter because you too are not from this place, and you too find the spectacle of fire amaaazing, though you know enough not to smile so dotish and look so stupidly impressed by it. And you suspect as well that there is a layer of meaning that the North-erners not seeing quite yet, and maybe won't ever see at all—a layer of jumbie and spirit and all that is bodiless. And is OK. Is OK because Carnival is not a selfish country. Is a generous space. It can mean plenty things to plenty people. Is enough that you can see this aspect of spirit. You realise Carnival is a kind of country like this—where there is a mix up of people from every nation, and a mix up of races, and a mix up of classes—but also a mix up of the living and the dead, and the seen and the unseen, and the real and the unreal.

*   *   *

Being a supernatural creature—a squat, leprechaun-like figure from the forests of Guyana, a devious shape-shifter—I think it might have been OK for the buck to have appeared during Carnival; I think there might have been space even for misbehaving ghosts such as he. Especially this year. To my own ear, the sound of Carnival was changing. Is like something older and deeper was waking up. "This Carnival have a different kinda energy!" Machel Montano sang in the song he initially hoped would have been the anthem for 2019 and eventual Road March winner. I listen to him at his album launch. "Low! Low! Low!" he instructing the band the way Jamaican DJs instruct their bands when they want to bring the music down so they can talk to the crowd. Machel put his foot on a speaker and he talking like a high priest to his congregants. "My job," Machel say, "is to make you jump out of yourselves." And I think this thing he trying to articulate is so much bigger than any of our mouths can say, how in that country called Carnival you can be yourself and not yourself, and how it make space for jumbies and duppies to roam. I realise Machel is a man who take his job serious—who understand the kind of energy music supposed to create, and what it supposed to make possible, and he trying his best to create that energy.

Old people say man plan but God wipe. "Release" never gained the traction Machel was hoping for, and yet it still rang out like prophecy. 2019 Carnival really did have a different kind of energy, and Machel was in the middle of it like always. The song he wanted to win never win, but is only because he end up beating his own self. A collaboration between Bunji, Skinny Fabulous and Machel, a song called "Famalay", had the different kind of energy people was needing. It had the sound of Bouyon coming in from Dominica. And 2019 was also the year where other sounds from other islands was coming in. It was a year for the Jab-Jab sound as well—from Mr Killa's "Run Wid It" to Mandella Linkz's "Tombstone" to Lil Natty and Thunder's "Get in Your Section" and "Pandemonium" from Voice. That Jab-Jab sound from Grenada was invoking a different kind of mas—Spice Mas and Oil Mas—something grittier, dirtier, more primordial. And is not that Jab Jab wasn't just as native to Trinidad, or that the sound of it wasn't still there in the voice of Super Blue and the music of 3 Canal, but these was feeling more and more like exceptions. The majority of songs that were produced for Carnival had become so studio-perfect, such slick productions that they could feel as pretty and as tailored as Tuesday Mas. But this year it had a feeling like while the pious Christians had left for Tobago, Jab Jab had returned with this kind of grunting sound, a kind of growl, and I think maybe the buck could have found his rightful section, could have found his perfect direction in the midst of that. But the buck end up waiting for Carnival to done. He wait for the bands to be disbanded, and the J'Ouvert paint to be washed off the roads. It was a good two weeks after Carnival and no one was in the mood for bucks.

But this is not quite true. By all accounts not only had the buck been active during Carnival but from long before. He had been tormenting his chosen family in Gasparillo for all of seven months. It is not that the buck did not appear until after Carnival, but that the story of his haunting only made headlines after. A full two weeks after. Now all over Trinidad people was picking up the *Guardian* and reading this article, and then they put down the newspaper and they place their hands on their heads like they feel a migraine coming on. They shake those same heads wondering if they really and truly did read the story they think they did just read. They pick up the newspaper one more time to confirm that there, in black and white, was a genuine John 3: 16 article about a squat, leprechaun-like figure haunting Krishna and his poor wife, Balmattee, to the point where the buck even asking Balmattee for sex, and Balmattee feeling all frazzled and bothered and is now at her wit's end. Krishna at his wit's end as well. And their son Govinda, who can show you on his foot a red mark where the buck did attack him, is also at his wit's end. What to do? Hindu pundits, Christian preachers, Spiritual Baptist leaders, Orisha priests—they all arriving at the house in Gasparillo to perform exorcism, to anoint the doors with John-the-Conqueror oil and Run-Devil-Run, and to prove amongst themselves whose god is really the strongest. But this buck out to prove that he bigger and badder than any oil they can pour, than any god they can call upon. Police come to the house as well, not with oil, but with batons and with guns. But listen nuh—this buck badder than priest, him badder than preacher, him badder than pundit, and him badder than police.

Now the story of the buck creating its own little bacchanal all over Trinidad. More news teams going in. Camera crew going in. A fellow with a real sense of humour and satire write a story in the papers, an exclusive interview with the buck. People watching the news. They reading the articles. They reading the exclusive interviews with the buck. The buck say he is misunderstood. The buck say he want justice. The buck say he want less of whatever discriminatory ism it is that people practise against ghosts. People can't stop shaking their heads. People now laughing till their sides hurt, but they also frowning. They asking, "Is this what journalism has really come to in Trinidad?" And when they take to social media to talk bout this buck (which is how I hear bout it in the first place) they using the hashtag #TrinidadIsNotARealPlace.

I think is plenty, plenty things to unpack from that hashtag. #TrinidadIsNotARealPlace. By which I think they mean to express a kind of incredulity. By which I think they mean to say, *lawd these people can embarrass you eh!* By which I think they mean, this run of articles in the Trinidad *Guardian* would not have happened in the UK *Guardian*, or in *The New York Times*, or in any "real" newspaper. By which I think they was probably thinking again about those Northerners who had come down for Carnival—the self-same ones who had been smiling so dotishly and taking pictures of the fire-breathing woman—they was imagining them reading the story of the buck and squinting their eyes and asking "Wha' de ass is a buck?" but in their own accents, and they were feeling themselves judged by such questions. Not just Trinidadians but all of us across the Caribbean—we were feeling ourselves judged by such imagined questions. By which I do not think we were saying that we don't believe in the supernatural—in what Toni Morrison calls the world beyond the five senses—in jumbies, and jab jabs, and even bucks—but that there is a time and place. I find myself wondering bout time and place. Does time and place exist only for a week? When is the time and place to talk bout unrealities in the Caribbean that so often feel like realities, or the time to talk bout the bodiless, or the things that can change their bodies and therefore change the meanings.

All across the Caribbean we know this to be true—that the crossroads is a powerful place, an intersection not just of streets, but of the real and the unreal. It is at the crossroads that you might buck up on a jumbie, or a duppy, or a buck for that matter. Thinking bout it now, I realise is true. Marching on that J'Ouvert morning, it was always at the crossroads that the woman with her torch would get into a kind of spirit and make her circle and breathe out that breath of fire. It was at the crossroads that we was always finding spirit. As I read more bout this buck that is raining down hell on poor Krishna and Balmattee and Govinda, I think that he might be his own crosses and his own crossroads—his own intersection of the Caribbean, and our histories and tensions that live with us and between us even today.

In Guyana the name is not buck but "bacoo". They believe this comes from the Yoruban legend of the Abiku—a spirit baby who end up dead before he even get a name. Or else it could come from the word "Baku", which in some West African languages means "little brother" or "short man". The Guyanese bacoo can be a terror, but if you know the way to trap him in a bottle, he can also grant your wishes. There are stories of Trinidadians who have gone to Guyana, lost themselves in the hinterland, on the hunt for their own bacoo that they believe would be the key to wealth. By the time the bacoos, trapped in their bottles, get to Trinidad, the name get shorten down to "Buck". And so this is the creature, by way of Guyana, by way of Nigeria, who they say is now haunting a family in Gasparillo.

Things get even stranger. Krishna say the buck has been speaking to his family at night. Krishna say the buck has been threatening them in a blood-curdling, demonic voice. Krishna say he have the evidence! He have a recording of the buck. Krishna plays the tape. On the tape the buck sound evil for true, even if a little cartoonish. And it have cats yowling in the background like is Halloween. The buck giving real robber-talk on that tape. He boasting bout what he going to mash up and what he going to destroy and who and who he don't fraid. And then the buck claim his nationality, his specific place in the world. Listen nuh—this buck say he don't come from Trinidad. And he don't come from Guyana either. Neither did the buck travel all the way from the African continent. The buck say he come from Jamaica. It is a Yardie buck who grow up on ackee and cornmeal dumpling. I scratch my head hard at that one. I start to laugh. I thinking bout the different duppies we have in Jamaica—Rolling Calf, Ol'Higue, River Mumma and that East Indian duppy whose name is offensive outside of our shores. But I never once hear bout no "buck". I know bout "bull buck and duppy conqueror" but that is not a duppy—just somebody who so strong and confident that they not afraid of bulls or duppies. But here is this buck claiming my own country even as he doing it in a Trini accent. Listen to what the buck say on the tape: "I doh fraid Pundit Ramesh . . . and I doh fraid no pastor!"

It take me a minute before I finally understand that "Jamaica" in the buck's mouth don't quite mean Jamaica. It does not signify the country, but instead, the body. It is a signifier of blackness, and a kind of badman-ness, and a kind of ruthlessness. I feel a heaviness when I realise this and I understand now that the story of the buck is frivolous but not frivolous at all.

Sometimes when we tell the story of the Caribbean, we tell it as a simple story with only two characters: whiteman versus blackman. But in truth it had so many other bodies having so many other interactions and producing so many other stories. Who will tell the story of the black woman and the Indian man, or the Taino man and the Chinese Man, or the Syrian woman and the Chinese woman, and so many other combinations, and alliances, and betrayals, and children who had inherited these conflicting histories? And how is it that even today we still so suspicious of each other? What stands between our ability to love each other if not these hardly ever told stories that come back to haunt us as bucks? I wonder what it mean for this Indo-Trinidadian family to be haunted by an Afro-Jamaican ghost? I want to tell Bal-mattee I take no responsibility for the buck, but I sorry for the history that haunts her. I sorry for the histories that haunt all of us. I so sorry for all them things that we find difficult to face or to talk about because we wish they wasn't real, just like we sometimes wish this place wasn't real and that our history wasn't real, and that the present wasn't real, and that the things that haunt was just a figment of our overactive imaginations.

And I think how sweet J'Ouvert morning was this year— how we was walking in that before-day-morning. How some of us came out as bats, and some of us as devils, and some of us as just ourselves because sometimes that is the hardest mas to play. And I remember how we anointed each other with paint and mud and glitter because this was ritual. And I remember the fire coming out of the woman's mouth and the heat that was on our skins. And I remember how we was chipping by the cemetery and how after a while it did feel like things from the cemetery was chipping right behind us. But it was nothing to be afraid of. It was OK. We was as fearless as that Jamaican buck in Gasparillo. And I remember the North Americans who was taking pictures, but how their cameras couldn't capture all that was happening in that rising dawn. For there was things there you could see and other things you could not see. And in this mix of tourist and local, jumbie and human, the bodied and the bodiless, I think I don't know any time or place more real.

8

OUR WORST BEHAVIOUR

Now everyone jump up and show me
your worst behaviour
Just show me your worst behaviour
Wine up with your worst behaviour
Start the bacchanal!

—Skinny Fabulous

Carnival in Trinidad has a particular and layered history. It is a wild story that involves French planters sailing from the Old World to the New and then from island to island, trying to outrun revolutions—first the one in France, and then the one in Haiti, but no matter how far they ran, a revolution would eventually find them; it involves enslaved people and their emancipation and burning stalks of sugar cane (cannes brûlées) held high above their heads; it involves stick fighters and chantwell singers who would evolve into calypsonians and then later into soca artists; it involves riots and a brutal militia and at least one young man dying while two of his friends are taken to hospital.

The history of Jamaica Carnival is much thinner. The event is still seen by many as a poor facsimile of the real thing that takes place in Trinidad and Tobago. History, however, only requires the passing of time, one year stacked upon another, and someone to document it. So then, let this moment be recorded—that in Jamaica, in the Road March of 2013, an incident happened that caused such a scandal across the island that for days people wrote furious letters to the newspapers or called in to one of the island's daytime radio talk show programmes, each of them—the letter-writers and the callers —frothing over themselves to see who could express the greatest outrage.

Something of the sort had happened before in Trinidad. After Emancipation when the French planters saw black bodies include themselves in what had been their own private revelry, they filled the *Port of Spain Gazette* with pronouncements of disgust:

"Diabolical!"

"All immorality and no refinement!"

"Wretched buffoonery!"

"An annual abomination!"

Island to island, carnival to carnival, this history has repeated itself. In 2013, Carnival spectators in Jamaica watched in horror as bodies that they would have preferred sidelined, included themselves in the masquerade, and by the inclusion of their spectacular bodies, they changed the meaning of the mas.

The Fete

On sabbatical from the UK-based university where I work, I spend the first half of 2013 back in Jamaica. I have landed a gig as a visiting professor at the university here. It is not onerous work. Once a week I teach a workshop. I spend the rest of the days trying to finish a novel I have been working on. On the weekends I make the most of the Carnival season.

Carnival builds to its crescendo over several weeks. Today, fetes happen in venues across Kingston, but in 2013 they were mainly held in the shadow of the National Stadium at a venue called Mas Camp. You might think of these parties as events that, over the weeks, grow in number and intensity and anticipation. The music from the parties spills out over the city. The parties grow until they can no longer be contained in a single venue and so they spill out onto the road. The road is the ultimate expression of carnival. Revellers enter the road as one might enter a temple—the holy space we have waited on all year.

In February, there are still eight weeks left to wait for the road but Mas Camp is already heaving. It could worry you a little to see the hundreds of cars parked outside the venue knowing that in about four or five hours their drivers will be a little intoxicated. Breathalyser tests had been introduced to the island years before but most have fallen into disuse and are rusting away in some government storeroom. The worst of the drivers will sleep in their vehicles for an hour or so before driving home, but most will simply switch to water in the final hour of the party and dance harder as if to sweat out the alcohol. Walking through the parking lot towards the fete, the cars are making their own music—the expensive models beeping a warning any time someone gets too close to them. This has been one of the most enduring criticisms of Jamaica Carnival, the class lines that it erects, as if what Jamaica has inherited is the elite Carnival of the French planters and not the one that had been transformed after Emancipation.

Inside the venue, I go to the bar first. Apple vodka and Ting. I find my "crew" in the usual spot, a loose arrangement of friends and acquaintances. I raise a cup to them and they slur their greetings. An all-inclusive party, the ground is already littered with cups. Perhaps it is that soca music requires more reckless abandon than the more popular reggae or dancehall events across the island. We dance. The DJ plays the opening strains of one of the hits of the season, Patrice Roberts's "A Little Wine":

Everyboooodddy! Wine on somebody now!
Take a wine, everybody!
Wine on somebody now.
A little wine never hurt nobody.

For all the wildness of a soca event, patrons are famously obedient to the instructions contained in the songs. *Get something and wave!* Or *Drop on the ground and roll!* Or *Pick up something, anything, now run with it!* So if Patrice Roberts is telling us to dance against somebody now, even with a stranger, that is exactly what we will do. Across the party people are pairing up and sometimes tripling up. I am grabbed from behind by a woman I don't know, but it is OK; this is soca. We are inside the music. I look behind to see that she is almost as tall as me and wider. She takes a handful of my dreadlocks and pushes my face down towards the floor. My body is a loose puppet as she presses her pelvis into me. This kind of role reversal is possible in a fete—the woman as the more aggressive dance partner. As she dances against me and my face is still pointing towards the ground, I can only see the feet of other patrons as they walk by. One pair of feet stops in front of me. I look up and into the stunned face of a girl no more than eighteen or nineteen. I think I recognise her but I am not sure. She manages to say, "Dr Miller!?"

Now I remember. She is one of my new workshop students at the university. She giggles and walks away as if she has discovered one of my dirty secrets. I am only a little embarrassed. The message contained and repeated in almost every soca song is clear: *Show me your worst behaviour! Get on bad! My pride is in the "Lost and Found"! Misbehave!*

The criticism of Jamaica Carnival as an exclusive event is fair, but on those Friday nights at Mas Camp, it was impossible not to see the opposite as well—a kind of inclusiveness. Here was a music that refused to judge its patrons, that asked everyone, regardless of talent, to dance and be involved. It was nothing like reggae or dancehall. And here were DJs who did not shout over the microphone, as they did in dancehall, telling you all the reasons why you might not belong. *Hand in de air if you love God!* the dancehall DJ will shout, and you must put your hand in the air, even if you are an atheist. *Hand in de air if you never borrow gyal clothes!* And all women must immediately throw their hands in the air to prove their financial independence. They are wearing their own clothes.

Nothing has been borrowed. *Hand in de air if you never dash weh nuh belly!* Another instruction directed to women who must again throw their hands in the air to prove their virtue, that they have never had an abortion. *Hand in de air if yu love woman! We bu'N out all battyman!* This one for the men who must now lift their hands to declare their masculinity and their straightness.

All of this was absent from soca music, and this is what was brewing in Jamaica Carnival's 2013 season—a kind of inclusion that had once seemed impossible in Jamaica. What is simmering underneath the music is a distinctly queer possibility.

Beach J'Ouvert

It is only a week away now. As if to give the city a break, a chance to recuperate before the big road event next Sunday, the parties have migrated from Kingston to the north coast of the island. We are at James Bond Beach, named so because in the hills above here, the novelist Ian Fleming once came every winter to write another of his famous spy novels. His villa, Goldeneye, is one of the many that has been booked solid for the weekend as carnival revellers swarm the resort towns of Ocho Rios and Oracabessa.

Beach J'Ouvert starts early. The gates open at midday and not long after the party is already loud and full of laughter as if it has been going on for hours. The DJ is playing Fay-Ann Lyons's "Miss Behave". In the song she recalls Carnival the year before in which she had behaved badly. The new year finds her in a repentant mood. She sings how ashamed she is of the excesses to which she had given over. Restraint will be her goal this year. *I will behave this year! I will behave this year!* she sings over and over as if trying to convince herself. Her failing resolve is the whole energy of the song, and the crowd listening is happily failing with her.

> *I won't get mad, I won't get crazy,*
> *I won't get mad, I won't get crazy,*
> *I won't get mad, I won't get crazy . . .*
> *UNTIL I HEAR DEM SAAYYY . . .*

And now the song has reached its climax; everyone waits on the instruction. And she gives it:

> *Drop on the ground and roll!*
> *Drop on the ground and roll!*

The instruction is metaphorical—it imagines a woman lowering her knees (dropping on the ground) and gyrating her buttocks (rolling)—but everyone takes its first and most literal meaning. We drop ourselves in the sand or on the slightly muddy terrain of the grounds and roll about as if we have either found or lost religion. It carries on like this for hours. In between songs we dip into the blue waters of the Caribbean Sea to cool off. As sunset approaches, the water turns from blue to gold and I remember how this part of the island got its name—Oracabessa, from the Spanish, oro cabeza, golden head.

It is now 7 p.m. The party is in its last hours and it is time for the paint to come out. This is a J'Ouvert tradition. You must come prepared to get dirty. It is almost impossible to escape a J'Ouvert party without being splattered with paint and powder and mud, a kind of anointing. For protection, some of the women put shower caps they have brought over their hairdos. Buckets of red and green paint are passed around and before long it is being splattered all about. The paint splashing releases a new energy, a renewed sense of abandon. The DJ is playing a new song. I do not remember what song it is, but I remember what he shouts into the microphone: "People, this is the point in the party where anything goes!"

I wonder if I have heard him right. I wonder if I am too tipsy to understand his meaning. I look around me and my vision blurs a little. Everyone looks a little bit like everyone else. It isn't the alcohol. Under the dual covering of dusk and paint, gender has become ambiguous. Here it is—the queer possibility. This is what I see: a man a few yards in front of me makes his whole torso fall like the woman had forced me to do in Mas Camp weeks ago. He does it on his own though, head touching toes, and he starts to gyrate. Another man notices, approaches him from behind and starts to dance against him. The first man looks up. He squints, and for all of half a second he seems surprised. It is only for half of a second. He shrugs. This is Carnival. This is soca. This is a place for misbehaviour. He pushes himself against the dance partner. I had never seen this in Jamaica before—not in public. The erotic dancing between two men turns into a line of three, and then four, and then five—a conga line of sorts. I cannot help but feel a little afraid for them—the public display of it all. This is Jamaica, I want to say, but nothing happens. No one seems to care at all. I smile and raise my cup of apple vodka and Ting to the sky, toasting this island that has begun to change right in front of my eyes.

Later that night, back at the villa where I am staying for the night, I call a friend and narrate the evening to him. I think that he will be as pleased as I am—that he will comment on the way that Jamaica is slowly changing, making space for his own body—his own desire. I am mistaken. He sucks his teeth indignantly. *You see, that is the problem with soca!* he declares. *It just bring out the worst in us! That could never happen in dancehall!*

Road March

It is finally here. From around ten in the morning until six in the evening, the Carnival parade will wind its way through the streets of New Kingston. It starts on Knutsford Boulevard, then Trafalgar Road passing the British High Commission, then Hope Road passing Devon House and the Bob Marley Museum and back. Two sets of people have come out for the event—the participants, all decked out and who leave in their wake bits of feathers and sequins that have fallen from the costumes; as well, there are the spectators who line each side of the streets who have just come out to watch. Between the revellers and the spectators is a line of security who have formed themselves like a chain gang, long metres of rope held in their hands to maintain the separation. In Trinidad where this practice developed, a few carnival bands have held out and refuse to march with this kind of security. The separating rope, they argue, is too powerful a symbol of other divisions. It is against everything that Carnival means. They say, *if a man from the crowd catch the spirit and feel to dance, then let him dance, because that is holy.* They say, *if a man feel a vibe to march with you for a mile then let him march with you for a mile, because that is brotherhood.* Some say, *the road belongs to no one;* others say, *it belongs to everyone.* They are saying the same things.

What happened in Jamaica in 2013 is this: a few boys of disrepute (to put it plainly, they were transgendered) were lured in by the music. They rose out of the gullies in which they had been forced to live and they danced behind the music trucks, a little further back from the band as if they were its glamorous tail. Look closely; you should recognise some of these boys. O'Neil and Saville are amongst them. They are the same ones from the harbour—the Gully Queens. They had already gained a reputation in Kingston. They were prostitutes; they bleached their skins; they squatted in abandoned houses in nice neighbourhoods. In the nice neighbourhoods, they did not keep quiet. They had arguments and the sound travelled over fences and into the living rooms of the well-to-do. They stole items of clothing from off the line after the maids had put them out to dry. At first, Missus had even accused the maids despite tearful protestations. The truth made no sense—not at first. The items that were stolen were skirts and little dresses and lace panties. They could not imagine men stealing such things. These were the boys who came out on Sunday to play mas.

"Diabolical!"

"All immorality and no refinement!"

"Wretched buffoonery!"

Whenever I apply a soundtrack to this moment, I play "Behaving The Worst" by Skinny Fabulous:

> *Out of all ah mi friend dem,*
> *I cause the most problem!*
> *I come to start the bacchanal!*

That is ahistorical; Skinny's anthem, this championing of outrageous behaviour, would actually be released six months later, in time for the 2014 season. Still, I bring it forward the way the boys brought their bodies forward and offered them to the mas.

Some spectators were visibly upset. They muttered amongst themselves. They spat on the ground. Then, a few decided to make their objections known more forcefully. The Gully Queens were only dancing but suddenly stones were being thrown at them. It surprises me even now that they did not flinch at the attack. They had already learned the lesson; there is only one way to deal with a bully even if, sometimes, that bully feels like an entire island. You must stand your ground. Well, they did more than just stand. They took up the stones that had landed at their feet and hurled them back into the crowd. They hurled them with as much conviction and as much defiance as they could summon, and a whole new bacchanal began.

People were shouting. People were scattering in all directions. I do not know how the Gully Queens escaped, only that they did. Perhaps they were as good at fighting as they were at fleeing, and they knew instinctively when to do what. One woman had to be carried off to the hospital for stitches; one of the flung stones had opened up her forehead. It was for the sake of this woman that all the furious letters were sent in to the newspapers and all the angry calls made to the radio stations. *Imagine that! The poor woman didn't do anything! Was just out to enjoy a peaceful Sunday and look how she end up with a buss-up head, all because of those perverts!*

I learned a new word in the hullabaloo: obstreperous— resisting control or restraint in a difficult manner; unruly; noisy, clamorous, or boisterous; bad behaving. On a *Jamaica Gleaner* online forum, one brave respondent going against the crowd dared to express sympathy for the Gully Queens and what had driven them to defend themselves. He was promptly dismissed by another respondent:

You have not seen the way these men act. It's beyond outrageous. They taunt the crowd. Some take off their clothes and make lewd, suggestive and VERY unwanted gestures. I can't even express the scene I saw when I was out on Saturday night. And they just LOVE an audience. It's pure performance, so I can just imagine how they behaved on Sunday! Their obstreperous actions go way beyond demanding rights and equality.

The Gully Queens had behaved no more outrageously than we had at Beach J'Ouvert the week before. They had not even danced against each other. They did not need to. The offence they caused was in their own bodies. It was the way they walked in their bodies, and the way they danced in their bodies. And also, it was because they were poor.

We had all behaved our worst that day. The boys had. And the spectators had. And even the revellers had, for we simply marched onwards, along the sequin-strewn road, ignoring the fracas behind us as if nothing would spoil our fun. And also, we behaved at our worst in the days that followed when no word of empathy towards the boys would be tolerated, as if we were not allowed to understand them, let alone love them, let alone lift the rope that tried to separate us and invite them into the mas.

9

THERE ARE TRUTHS HIDDEN
IN OUR BODIES

I t is always the body that I return to—our bodies and their various meanings.

This is what happened: in the winter of 2004, a woman enters a shop in Manchester, England. It is a student shop attached to the student union and all the workers here either study at Manchester Metropolitan University or the University of Manchester. The vibe of the shop is a relaxed one, and the student workers have not only devised a rota for their work shifts and their lunch breaks, but also one for DJ privileges—each taking turns to play their music as it filters through the speakers of the shop.

The woman who has entered the shop seems to carry with her the weight of some deep annoyance. At the till she is unimpressed by the man (the man is me) who smiles brightly at her and asks, as he has been taught to, "Anything else for you?" There is something about her eyes and the curl of her lip that seems almost disgusted by him, but the man does not feel this is directed towards him. How could it be? What could he have done to earn such a visceral reaction by a stranger? She does not answer his question with words, but with a sort of twitch of the head signals, no, no . . . nothing else. I just want to leave. As the man scans and cashes her goods and then sorts out her change from the ten-pound note she has handed him, it seems the woman can finally hold it in no longer. "For godsake could you turn that music off! Don't you know how hateful it is?"

It is 2004. Terrifying stories have been leaking out about the violent homophobia on the island. Across England, Jamaican artistes are frequently being unbooked from shows after protest by LGBT rights groups accusing them of peddling hate music. In 2006 it will all culminate in an article in *Time* magazine declaring Jamaica "The Most Homophobic Place On Earth". It is only when the woman snaps, it is only when she asks, "Don't you know how hateful it is?" that the man (who is me) realises that he has been humming all along to the music in the background, that the rota says he has DJ rights for this hour and so he has been playing music from his island. It is only now that he listens more intently to the words of I Wayne singing "Lava Ground":

Deya pon de lava ground
An' nuff a dem ah look fi see I mawga down
hype pon warrior true dem have a gun
but tell dem seh de warriors naah guh run (naah guh run!)
Firm upon de lava ground.

A loose prose translation of the lines could be this: We are here on this troubled ground, and lots of people would love to see us diminished, they taunt us because they have guns, but tell them that we, the warriors, will not run. We will not run! We stand firm upon this troubled ground.

The man wonders what could possibly be seen as hateful in this declaration of defiance, this insistence on standing one's ground, this refusal to be intimidated even when we are approached with guns or with the threat of violence—this stance which has in fact been the stance of so many heroic LGBT Jamaicans? It takes the man a second—a solitary second of being reduced by the woman's stare, her clear repulsion of him and his body, to understand what she is hearing and understanding. She understands correctly that the music is Jamaican and she understands that the man is also Jamaican. She had observed him—his over-200-pound black, male body, his dreadlocks—and having read all the stories, she understands that Jamaica is a homophobic island and that much of its music stridently advocates for the killing of gay men. It stands to reason then—the big black man in front of her who is clearly the cause of this Jamaican music, who is singing along to it, must necessarily be humming a tune of hatred. If Jamaica is only defined by its homophobia, then every Jamaican must be either an agent of or a victim of such hate. She has, in her mind, some imagination of the broken, brown queer body. It is that body on whose behalf she believes she is now speaking. She does not imagine that the body before her is one such body. She does not understand that in the actual moment of encountering a brown, queer body from Jamaica, all she does is to berate that body and silence it. But because the customer is always white (or is it that the customer is always right? In that moment they mean very much the same thing) the man turns off the radio and hands his DJ rights over to another student worker whose music, being less black, will undoubtedly be less offensive.

This is also what happened: On a train from Heathrow Airport I sit across from two men who seem very much in love, and who it seems have flown across from America to England for a vacation. Their love is not the extravagant kind, but the deeper one that has settled into a comfortable place. They, almost unconsciously, touch each other often—a hand on the other's knee as they talk, or ask a question. A finger raised to the other's face to wipe away a ketchup stain. It is so sweet, I cannot help but smile.

One of the men looks up and catches me staring and his face turns into a scowl. "What?" he barks at me. "You got a problem with gay people!?"

I stammer. I turn away.

This is what has happened more times than I can count: it is close to midnight in Manchester, or sometimes London, and I am in a line outside inching towards a door. Whenever the door opens, the hard thump of a kind of techno beat leaks out into the street. My friends have decided on a "big night out". This will involve drinking and dancing into the wee hours of the morning. There are no women in this line, but some of the men are shivering in that same way you often see women shivering in lines outside of clubs, pulling the jackets of their boyfriends tight around them. The men who are shivering are sometimes shirtless—wearing just a pair of shorts and a leather harness around their chests. It is no wonder they are cold.

Finally, at the door, the bouncer—a man about 6-foot 5 and almost as wide—looks at me with a stern face. His sternness is not only reserved for me. It is the face he presents to everyone, but still it seems that he considers me for a longer moment, blocking my entrance.

"You know what kind of club this is?" he finally asks.

"Yes," I say.

"You sure you want to go in?" he asks.

"Yes," I say.

"I don't want any trouble," he says.

"Sure," I say.

This is a truth—a difficult and complicated truth: the place where I have always felt most comfortably gay is in Jamaica. In Jamaica, I know the language and the mannerisms of queerness. In Jamaica, I know how to dance. In Jamaica, I do not have to constantly translate my sexuality into mannerisms and speech and dances that sometimes feel to me, profoundly British. That sometimes feel profoundly white. In Britain I often have to dance my queerness to the hard thump of a techno beat. It is difficult to dance my queerness to soca or to dancehall or to reggae. In Britain, my black body often hides the truth of my queerness.

This is what happened: it is 6 August 2012—the fiftieth anniversary of Jamaica's independence. I am back in Glasgow. At this moment in time, Scotland is contemplating her own possible independence. In two years' time a referendum will be held on the matter, and though it will be unsuccessful, Glasgow as a city will vote overwhelmingly in favour of it. The mood, the appetite for an end to the British union is palpable in Scotland's largest city, so the African and Caribbean Society have convened a panel not only to celebrate Jamaica's independence but to ask what lessons Scotland might take from the island it once helped rule—an island that gained its independence as much from Scotland as it had from England.

An old man in the audience says he was a young British soldier stationed in Jamaica on 6 August 1962. He watched with tears in eyes as they raised the black, green and gold saltire flag over an independent country. He says, with a tremor in his voice, that there is nothing he would want more than to live to see the blue and white saltire raised over an independent Scotland. As someone else who has lived between Scotland and Jamaica, I have been brought in to moderate this panel.

After the old man has spoken, a much younger man in a blue plaid shirt raises his hand for the roving audience microphone to be passed to him. He stands and adjusts his glasses while reading from his notes, the telltale sign of a journalist preparing for an article. He asks, "But how can we celebrate Jamaica's independence when there is a whole section of the population who have never felt included as citizens?" The man in the blue plaid shirt has undoubtedly heard the worst stories, and though the worst stories are indeed the worst, it does not stop them from being true. He has read about gay

Jamaican men who have been run out from their houses, or who have been stoned, or who have been chopped with machetes and killed. Some have been lucky enough to jump on a plane and seek asylum elsewhere. The man in the blue plaid shirt cannot see into the future. He cannot know that in a year's time, on this exact day, the Jamaican reggae singer, Queen Ifrica, will be on stage at Jamaica's National Stadium and will pause her performance at this Independence event to celebrate the straight people present in the audience. Only the straight people. "Woman and man we say!" she will shout into her microphone. "No gays round here!" This would add to his point. There is another future he cannot see; in three years' time, on this exact day, Jamaica Pride will have its first successful staging. They will tie the idea of their own independence to the independence of the island, and this would subtract from the man's point.

Still, the man in the blue plaid shirt is not writing for the future; he is writing an article for an LGBT magazine today, and today his question is an urgent one. I would have liked to answer it myself—not that such questions can ever be properly answered, they can only be engaged with—but I remember that my role is to moderate. I dutifully pass the question over to the panel.

The panellists are all men. They all identify as straight. They are all black. They were born in the Caribbean or on the African continent. They speak with accents that belong to hotter climates. They are unprepared for this question. They hem and they haw. Their denunciation of the homophobia that too often defines black communities is neither fulsome nor convincing. Their answers satisfy neither me nor the man in the blue plaid shirt, who is once again on his feet, who has not yet given up the microphone, whose face is now flushed with a fury that reveals the piece he is writing is not just journalism but a cause that he genuinely believes in. He is shouting now, "Well quite frankly, if I was a gay man in Jamaica, I would want to kill myself!" And the statement slaps the air right out of me.

But I didn't want to kill myself; it wasn't like that! is what I want to shout back, except that isn't really the point. Except there would have been boys in Jamaica who had wanted to kill themselves, and some who had been successful—boys who had decided to be the orchestrators of their own deaths rather than give the pleasure to an angry mob. Of course this fact is not unique to my island—across the world the rate of suicides amongst LGBT youths is consistently higher than that of the general population. But to follow that line of thought is to go down the same road that the panellists before me had just fumblingly travelled. To travel that particular road is to be an apologist—to defend the indefensible.

No. It is something else. It is that the man in the blue plaid shirt is speaking for me. He is speaking on behalf of my body. It is that my body hides its truth from him. It is that his own body hides mine. It is that his genuine anger, the volume that he has brought to the microphone, depends on the silence of my body. It is that his words do not give voice to a voiceless community, but instead they *make* that community voiceless. It is that, although I am sitting on stage right in front of him, I am still only a figment of his imagination. It is that it is disturbing to watch someone trying to imagine the thing he does not know he is looking at. It is that he has become just another white man who can only imagine my body as dead or desiring death.

Of course, I do not say any of this. I do not think he wants to hear my truth. His anger and his righteousness are simple. Easy. The truth that my body hides is not. It is complicated. It is difficult. And I do not say my truth because it is too important.

10

THE WHITE WOMEN AND
THE LANGUAGE OF BEES

I
must be given words so that the bees
in my blood's buzzing brain of memory

will make flowers, will make flocks of birds,
will make sky . . .

– Kamau Brathwaite

I write a message to the white woman, though right now
I do not know if someone like me have the right words
to say to someone like she. I press "send" all the same. I think
that right now she might be hiding from a man. The man is
not me, but sometimes I think he may as well be me, which
is to say that he is tall and black and he write all kinda books
that try to capture the lushness and the harshness of these
rocks that we call islands that we call home. This man decide
to take it on himself to tell the white woman that she is not
one of us, that she don't speak for us or even to us. In fact,
he is quite surprised (this is what he tell she) whenever he
pick up a newspaper and see her face staring back at him.
He is surprised when him see people calling her a writer from

these rocks that we call islands that we call home. He want to know what someone like she could ever know about people like we, and about these rocks, and about these flowers, and about the language of bees. The man's words move sharp as a cutlass and open up an old wound on the white woman's skin. A world of anxiety festers in that wound.

I know that this man is just a carry-down artist. He see people trodding on whatever Zion-road they be trodding on, and he try to carry them down, even to carry them down to nothing. It is true that the white woman was not born on these rocks. She has this in common with the man—that they both live in places they were not born to. They are both immigrants. But the white woman has lived on these rocks for longer than he has lived away from them. And she has given birth on these rocks. And when she writes, she uses the range of languages and dialects that springs from these rocks. How many years and decades must pass before we can belong to a place and to its words? How much time before we can write it? In my message I tell the white woman that it is he—the carry-down man—who does not speak for us. He certainly don't speak for me. The white woman tells me how she did wake up that morning and place her head under a tap of water and she just stay there while the hand of the clock moved itself from morning to lunchtime. She let the water beat over her head and I do not know whether this was some sort of punishment or just a way to wash away the awfulness of the carry-down man's words.

She say to me, Kei—look at me. I weigh 400 pounds. I cannot hide. And she say it as if pounds was the same as years, like she was saying, I weigh 400 years—as if hers was the entire weight of our history, of cane fields and the Atlantic. And also, she ask me, what is the raasclawt language of bees? I wonder to myself what kind of man could make a woman feel so bad bout herself—could leave her numb by a tap of water considering how she might fit herself down the drain. And I can't find the tongue to say O Daughter of Zion, lift up thine head. For yours is the weight of love and livity. Four hundred pounds is the weight of 20,000 hibiscuses, or better yet, the weight of 1.3 million bees—the weight of venom you should have applied to the man.

In truth, the white woman don't need my help nor my benevolence. Perhaps that is my own arrogance—a lesson that I too have to learn. Still, I tell the white woman what little words I have to say and she tell me thanks and that my words mean something. But in time it is she who will pick her own self up, and it is she who will find her own tongue in her own mouth and will say, "Daughter of Zion . . . Daughter of Zion . . . Daughter of Zion," and she will say it until the words create a kind of energy and the energy lift her right back to her own Zion-road, and along that Zion-road she find a poem and then another poem and then another, and the poems will build up one by one to form a whole new book, and the book will be a thing indisputably of the rock. It is she—the white woman—who will recognise the man not for his blackness nor for his manness but for what is fragile and tremulous underneath it all.

*   *   *

I sit down to read the latest book of the white woman. No. It is not the same white woman. I know that sometimes it could seem that way, which is the whole point of this thing. At the same time that I read the latest book of the white woman, the white woman is reading my latest book (I know this because she has said as much) and I think it is a funny thing this, to live simultaneously in each other's words. I must say that I feel relieved that I like the white woman's book. For true, she understands the lushness and the ugliness of these rocks, and sometimes she describes things in such a way that make me see a landscape I have always known, but in a whole different light. This land is hers too, and also the water. She knows better than me the direction of rivers, and the colours that play on its surface. She knows the names of things—of trees and flowers and vines that grow along the bank of the river, and the peculiar shape of the roots. She knows the quality of heat that wraps itself around everything like a blanket. I find myself thinking that this is some of the best writing I have read from the white woman, and yet still I have questions. Yet still, something feel wrong.

All of this keen observation is coming out of the mouth of a man that the white woman has invented. According to the white woman's invention, this man have no education to speak of. So how is he speaking these things? It is not that I don't believe that such a man would observe all the things that he observes, but I do not believe the language of his observation. I feel like the white woman has not trusted the eloquence of her own character—has not imagined him as a man capable of saying the things she would like him to say but in his own way. It is as if she grew frustrated and decided to put his own voice to the side and put her own white woman's voice in his mouth. This land is hers too, and also the water, and also the language.

This thing is complicated. It is not that I believe that a writer—the novelist to be specific—must be some kind of sociolinguist. I do not believe that the writer must make people say exactly the things that they would usually say. That is a kind of laziness, a dereliction of duty. I believe something else entirely. I believe the novelist must sometimes give to their characters things to say that they are fully capable of saying, but which they might not have thought to say themselves. In this way writing can give itself back to people and extend them. So I sit there reading the white woman's book that has been written so beautifully, but is not the voice of the man who saying all these beautiful things. It is not *his* beauty—for I know this man, and I know he has his own beautiful way of seeing and saying things.

I wonder why the white woman hasn't given herself access to this man's voice, or given the man access to his own voice and his own possibilities. Maybe the white woman has her reasons, and maybe they are very good reasons, but suddenly is like I feel the hand of the white woman as she is writing the very page that I am reading, as if I have stepped through some portal of time, and is like I notice that her hand is trembling. Was she really afraid? Was she nervous about people like me reading her book and throwing words like "appropriation" about? Am I a part of her anxiety?

I think all these things but I do not know how to say any of it to the white woman. Would she be defensive? Worse, would she see me as yet another tall, black man attacking her and questioning her rightful place in this world? No. I would not want to make her feel like that, so I say nothing. And my mind run again on Dionne Brand's essay—how race mediates all our exchanges, how there are some things we can say and other things we cannot say. And always, the most important things are the things we cannot say.

I am with the white woman who once again is not the same white woman. It seem an obvious thing to say, but sometimes we must say the obvious: not every white woman is the same white woman; and not every black man is the same black man. Our racial identities matter, but plenty times it is the personalities behind those identities that matter even more. It is our personalities that make us use our black-man-ness or our white-woman-ness in such different ways, as shield and as spear.

So me and this white woman are on a beach on an island in the Caribbean, and here it don't seem that night falls so much as it rises out of the water and then covers everything. I ignore the mosquitoes and my eyes are trained on the beach and to the darkening. I am here to see something I never seen before. I feel glad that the white woman has taken me here. As the waves tumble into the sand, so do the turtles. They allow themselves to be pushed in by the salty current of their own world. They are huge—these turtles—leatherbacks. The small ones weigh 400 pounds, and they get much bigger still.

All day I had caught glimpses of them, out there in the deep water, every now and then raising their snake-like heads up for a breath. They were waiting for the night—for this moment when they allow themselves to be pushed onto land. They look like dinosaurs to me—like something prehistoric— the way they lumber out of their wet world and how on land they seem to lose all of their grace. In water they move like ballerinas. On land, they are clumsy, hauling their bulk to some spot along the beach where they can dig their deep holes and lay their hundred or so eggs. They fall into a trance when they do this and you can even touch them if you want to, but I do not. Even gazing at them with the white woman, observing their ancient ritual feels like an intrusion of sorts, like we have let ourselves into a woman's birthing bed.

Some of these turtles have not been back to this land—to this particular beach—for thirty years. They were too busy growing up in the waters of Canada. The waters of North America have been kind to them. They have settled there. It is only the need to give birth that pulls them back to the very beach where they had been born years ago. In the time in between they have not visited—but when they become full of their eggs and of the future, something like the cord of love pulls back. They will trust their eggs to no other sand but the one found on these rocks that we call islands that we call home. These are the original natives. These are the original immigrants. They do not worry or politicise their various migrations. They simply are.

Have you ever witnessed the tears of turtles? It is a well-known phenomenon that when they come onto land they seem to cry—not no cow-bawling mind you. The beach isn't suddenly full of the sound of wailing. This is just a polite drop of water moving down their eyes as if these mothers are experiencing all the pain and joy of homecoming. We are told now that there is no emotion attached to this eyewater. It is just biology—the removing of excess salt from their bodies, and also a way to protect their eyes from the sand. The white woman beside me however is really crying. Real tears. Real emotion. She is upset by a man who is not me, but it may as well have been.

The man had written this thing about the white woman and his words had moved like a cutlass, but it was many years ago and I am surprised that the white woman is still so upset by it. She cries as if this thing had happened yesterday. I know I do not have the right to say how long pain should last, or what we have the right to be upset about, but these days I find it harder and harder to extend sympathy to the white woman. I cannot find in me the tongue to say, *Daughter of Zion, lift up thine head*, because—*Lord forgive me*—I do not think of her as a Daughter of Zion. I think she is Daughter of another place.

Like the sea turtles, she too had migrated. And then she started writing these books, and they were very good books. She had been back before—often—but now she came back as a writer and seemed to discover so many things about the selfsame place where she had been born. The white woman wrote an article about this coming back, about finding out to her great surprise that on these rocks that we call islands that we call home that there were actually writers. Who would have believed such a thing? Writers who live on rocks! And not only that—some of them were actually quite good!

One could have read the white woman's article for its generosity, or else one could have read it for its ignorance. The man had read the article for its ignorance and he had frowned. For days he had walked around with something like an annoyance growing inside him. It is true that the man was young—that age where things can seem to be more than they really are. The woman had written an article that few people would have read or even remembered, but the man had read it, and his annoyance grew and grew.

He thought about this white woman who was born on these rocks but who had become a writer elsewhere and so did not seem to know things. He could not forgive the white woman for her naïveté. His annoyance grew and became its own article. His article was many times larger than the small stub the white woman had written. In the man's article he calls the white woman a modern-day Columbus, for she had discovered what was already there.

Upon reading this, the white woman had cried for days and days, and even years later sitting on a beach and watching the turtles, she is still crying. She tell me again how the wicked man has ruined her. She tell me again that what the wicked man has written is libellous. She tell me again that she was tempted to file a big fat lawsuit gainst the man, but I think whichever lawyer she did talk to and who tell her that such a case was winnable was a samfy man, a merchant of snake oil, who did only want to take away what little money the white woman did have in her pockets. In any case, I glad she did not sue, for how would that have looked? A white writer from foreign sues a black man in the Caribbean—for what? Forgetting his place? Because he had the audacity and was renk enough to roll up all his smallness and blackness and use it as a weapon against her? She would not have survived the backlash.

There was a time when I did sympathise with the white woman who is also my friend. I used to tell her *yes, yes, the man's words were harsh* . . . because they really was harsh, but then I would add softly . . . *even though they were true. You understand that, right? There was truth in his words.* She didn't ever hear the last part. I suspect now, she could hear little beyond the sound of her own heart breaking. Every year I would try to say it a little bit louder: *there was truth in the man's words. You hurt him too! Do you understand that? You hurt him. You hurt me!* But she would never hear that sentence. She did not know how to.

All those plenty years ago when this thing started, I used to stay on the phone while the white woman cried and cried and one time she did tell me, brazen-like, that the problem with Caribbean literature is all the men. Is all those blasted black men who walk bout like them is some kind of king. And I did swallow at the other end of the line wondering if maybe she did forget who she was talking to—and wondering if she really thought that every white woman was the same white woman, and every black man was the same black man.

While the night rises up and the turtles lay their eggs, I tell the white woman, *Look nah! There are so many things we need to sort through and so many things we need to think through.*

There are so many conversations we still need to have, and many of them will not be polite. We not always going to play nice. But we must talk the things all the same. What we cannot do is throw a tantrum every time someone say something that get under our skin.

The white woman says, *That is all well and good for you to say, but talk to me when you too have been bullied by a black man. Talk to me after a man has aimed a steamroller at you and made you into nothing.* I think about these words. I think about this depiction of the black man as bully, as savage, as brute. And I think of the man who had frowned at the white woman's words and who in turn had strong words for the white woman, but how this man was really just a young writer from a small place who understood the largeness of his heritage. I think of what the white woman does not know, and what I do not know, and what she will never grasp, and what I will never grasp—what it means to be black in this world, what it means to be a woman in this world—and I think about the distance that will always be between us. I think too about the white woman who had placed her head under a tap of water. Things is never straightforward. Sometimes a man like me will wield words against the white woman, and the blade of those words are sharpened by the stone of his own insecurities, but another time the man will wield words against the white woman, and the blade of these words are sharpened by the stone of truth.

"Did I really deserve that? Am I such an awful person?" the white woman is pleading with me. I swallow something in my throat. Is she still looking for my help and benevolence?

I know she is not an awful person. She is like all of us. Sometimes there is goodness in her heart and sometimes there is darkness; I have seen both. But still and all, I think these questions are unfair. This thing have nothing to do with who deserves what, or being an awful person. And I think of how she so easily imagines the black man as a brute and a bully and a savage. I suspect it is the way she thinks of me when it suits her. It is the way that the past is always present. I feel the salt gathering in my own eye and so turn back to watch the turtles.

There was once a white woman who wrote a book about white women who were from these rocks and the book became very famous indeed. That white woman has died— though even now whenever we see Mad Bertha burning her- self up in the flames of Thornfield, we can't help but think *Antoinette! What a way them do you wrong, Antoinette!*

That famous book begins like this: *They say when trouble comes close ranks, and so the white people did.*

Today, a white woman is running through the streets of a nameless Caribbean island and shouting, *Close ranks! Close ranks!* And I wonder if maybe she has read the famous book but not understood it completely—its implicit critique.

Whatever the case, the white woman is running through the streets but no one is bothering with her. They not batting an eyelid. It is like people saying to themselves, Oh God! This again! She again! I cannot bother with she and she mad- ness today. And so as the white woman runs and her feet grow weary she find herself getting angry at all the tall white gates with all the good good white people behind them, and how none of them have come out to close ranks behind her.

The next day, this is what the white woman says to the other white woman: Where were you? I was shouting and shouting for us to close ranks!

And this is what the other white woman responds: Wha' de ass!! We still playing that Mas? Nah! I not into that!

The white woman says: But I was being attacked! The critics came for me with sharp knives. And when one of us is attacked, all of us are attacked!

The other white woman says: Nah! When you is attacked it mean that you is attacked. It mean you have to ask yourself, what have I done? And you gots to put on your big girl pants and your big girl shoes, and you parse out what is truth from what is fuckery and you deal with it.

The white woman says: But I was being attacked! The critics came for me with sharp knives. And when one of us is . . .

The other white woman interrupts: You listening to anything I saying, or you just going to repeat the same stupidness over and over?

The white woman says: But look at our skin! (and she puts her hand against the other white woman's hands, their freckles merging into one). We are sisters!

The other white woman says: Nah! That's not how this thing works. I am sister to everyone who is from these rocks and who sit down to try and write the lushness and ugliness of our existence.

The white woman takes out from her pocket a passport and says: Well then look! I am your sister. I am from here too.

The other white woman frowns: In a way, yes. But there is more. This thing have to do with more than just passports and birth certificates and the accidents of our birth. It have to do with the where that we choose, and the where that chooses us. It have to do with knowing the names of things. Of trees and flowers. It have to do with language. It have to do with knowing the word that we use is "sidewalk" and not "pavement", and that the word we use is "while" and not "whilst". You can't be writing this place and putting the wrong words in people's mouths. This rock is not made of granite or limestone, but with words. You must be given the right words. And these, my dear sister, are things you have yet to learn.

And when the other white woman says this, a swarm of bees rise up from a patch of yellow flowers, as if to say *yes, and yes, and Amen!*

The white women and I have things in common, bodies that are profoundly marked, though in different ways. One day I might admit this to the white women: *My dears, I know what it is to live in a body that is constantly marked as not belonging to the place in which it resides, but to tell the truth, I cannot comprehend the further pain of living in a body marked as not belonging even to the place to which it most profoundly belongs— marked as foreign even in its own home.*

The body of the white woman often gives her easy access to worlds for which I have no visa, but my own body gives me easier access to the words that make up my craft. We envy each other these things—these things that our bodies give us access to. If we could, would we trade our bodies, one for the other? I suspect not. So there is no real end to this, to this game, to this table that the black men and the white women dance around. Tomorrow there will be some new hurt, but who will cause it and who will nurse it is anyone's guess.

This evening, perhaps, the white women will find themselves sitting on rocks and looking out to the great expanse that is the Caribbean Sea. There are so many things in that sea like ships and their sad cargos, and the dying dolphins and the dying turtles and the dying sharks and all this damned dying that make the white women and the black men want to bawl together. And even the night that seems to grow large from all the relentless dying seems to rise out from the salty depths. And when the night rises and envelops everything, the white women, because they are writers, will grab hold of it and squeeze out their own small portion of ink. And if they are so lucky it will be that kind of night that buzzes like bees, and from its ink they will form words, and the words will form flowers that will form flocks of birds that will form sky.

II

DEAR BINYAVANGA, I AM NOT WRITING ABOUT AFRICA

(Binyavanga Wainaina, 1971–2019, was a Kenyan writer. He wrote the now famous essay, "How to Write About Africa" and the memoir One Day I Will Write About This Place.*)*

Dear Binj,

I am here, at last, because I promised.

No, that isn't quite true. In fact, it was you who promised to come to Jamaica, but then life happened, or more precisely, its opposite. You had your first big stroke. It was big enough that you actually noticed this one. Big enough that you ended up in hospital and big enough that you lost some of your speech. We all heard about it and so I adjusted our plans. If you couldn't come to Jamaica, then I would come to Kenya. So here I am, at last. It is almost a dozen months and a dozen strokes too late, and you are already dead.

Dear Binj,

I did not know that you were dying, or that you knew you were dying—and that you carried this around with you, this sense of the impending. Even then, when we met, the clock had already been set and was running down. How much time exactly was unclear. Five years—three years—a matter of months? Nothing specific. Only that you were not long for this world. American doctors told you to stay put in America, near to a hospital stocked with American medicine, and where they promised they had all the things that could keep your body going for as long as they could keep it going—which is a strange promise when you think about it, for everyone can promise at least that. You said naah anyway. You packed up and returned to Kenya. I get that.

Dear Binj,

I am here and writing to you and would like to assure you that I am not writing about Africa. I am only writing about myself in Africa—this place, this continent, where I think my body should make a kind of sense, but so far it doesn't make as much as I would like. I do not yet understand the end of that thought—only that it feels true and that there is some hurt at the end of the thought which I must face soon enough. I am starting here in Kenya, then I will go across the border to Ethiopia, and then I will fly all the way west, across to Ghana.

At Jomo Kenyatta International Airport, it isn't clear which line I should join. East Africans who do not require visas are directed to one line; foreigners who require visas are directed to another. I am neither fish nor fowl. I am not from East Africa, but my Jamaican passport means I do not need a visa. I ask the airport staff for help and am told to join the East African line. At the desk, the immigration officer looks at my passport and says, "Karibu"—the Swahili word for welcome, but I think he has said something like "Carib" or "Caribbean" and I stupidly say, "Yes, that's where I'm from." He looks at me oddly and shakes his head, but I don't think much of it at the time.

Outside, the driver who has my name written on a piece of paper says the word again, "Karibu", and then I see it written on a huge illuminated sign "Karibu Nairobi" and now I feel a little silly, but also a little pleased that this word for "welcome" should also name me and my place in the world.

Dear Binj,

I make a bad—an incredibly foolish decision. It is night and I use Google Maps to tell me the location of the pub where Wanjeri has said I should meet her. Wanjeri expects me to take a cab, but it is three kilometres away and I decide to walk it. I decide to walk it because I think it is a way to know a city, and I think I have gotten so fat over Christmas that I have been trying to walk everywhere. I see now that there's a way that someone like me, a black Caribbean man, can feel too comfortable in a city like Nairobi. So much reminds me of home.

What Google Maps tells me is this: that from the hotel to the pub is a walk of three kilometres, and that it is mostly flat, and that it should take me 37 minutes. As it often is in cities, I become the blue dot on my phone. I go where it tells me. There are other things that Google

Maps does not tell me. It does not tell me that the first two kilometres will be straightforward enough—will be along well-lit streets and parks, but the last kilometre will be along a major highway without streetlights. It does not tell me that the only footpath will be tucked away to the dark side of the road, that I will have to walk under bridges where the forgotten of this city seem to loiter and they will look at me suspiciously. It does not tell me—You are a foreigner! This is a bad decision! This is stupid! Run!

Wanjeri calls to ask where I am and I tell her. The call ends abruptly. Later she will tell me that she panicked but did not want to pass on that panic. And that she imagined my phone lit up in the dark and drawing even more attention to myself, and this was the only way she could think of to keep me safe—to end the call immediately.

I notice the boy who, from behind me, is walking at some speed. When he comes up to me and alongside me, he slows his pace—walking only a half a step in front of me. It doesn't take him long to turn around and ask me for money. He gesticulates from his hand to his mouth to indicate hunger. I say I don't have any money, and it helps that this is true. I do not so much see as I feel the presence of the other two boys who have come close behind me. It is almost impressive—the military tactic and precision, the way they have boxed me in. One of the boys behind, clearly to cause me some fear, keeps on saying, "No no. He looks like a good man. We do not need to kill him. We do not need to kill him." It is a game they have played before, and also it is not a game. The threatening words are meant to cause me panic, to make me become a useless fumbling thing, and they are working though I am trying hard to steel myself against their power. I think the boys are going to grab my bag and I decide that is fine. There is nothing much in it—nothing so irreplaceable. Instead, one reaches towards my back pocket, grabbing for my phone. I do not know why I do it, what instinct I am following, but I punch him in the face. He yells. I yell. We are looking at each other.

The way their eyes dart about me—I think I know what the boys are thinking. They are assessing me. My body. I am taller than they are. I am bigger than they are. I am suddenly grateful for my body and grateful for the weight that piled on over the Christmas. Still, I know that if they look at me for a second longer they will see right through me—they will see that I am soft, a foreigner with no fighting skills. In that split second, I run into the middle of the busy highway and stand between the cars zooming by. I yell some more. The boys are now surprised and seem to be considering not my body, but my mind. He is a crazy tourist. He is not worth it. I stay there in the road, flagging cars. The boys walk away slowly.

I run the last kilometre towards the pub. I stay in the road, on the far side. The drivers probably think me crazy, but I do not care. Along the way I pass at least two other groups of homeless boys—always in threes—and always pointing at me as if wondering if they should cross the road towards me.

The shock of the incident only grows the further I run away from it. Only now do I start to tremble. The trembling fills my body. *Shit*, I say. Over and over again. *Shit. Shit.* My body in this city feels profoundly unfamiliar, and noticeable, and vulnerable.

Dear Binj,

How did you become the kind of man that you became, and here? A big black man who began to wear pink tutu skirts just for the fuck of it. And did you not feel overly seen? Did you not feel vulnerable? And why did you return? I said before that I get it, and I think I mostly do, but sometimes I do not. When I talk about a place where our bodies make sense, what I really mean is a place where our bodies are not seen, where they raise no questions, where they are not worth pondering. I do not think I will ever have access to such a body again, not even in Jamaica. I wear the wrong clothes now, I am told, or the wrong jewellery. The sense of another place clings to me. And truth is, I would never want to fit in, not easily, even as I hate standing out. It is what it is.

Dear Binj,

The next evening I go to the launch of *Nairobi Noir*—a short story anthology—and I cannot help but think wryly that I have some qualification to be here, that I have some familiarity now with the dark underbelly of this city. The launch is held in the ground-floor auditorium of the Alliance Française, a theatre-like space, and it is a packed house—standing room only. It seems everyone who is a part of the Nairobi literary scene is here and so it hits me all over again

that you are not. Years ago, I had even written a story for
Kingston Noir when that globe-trotting anthology series had
dropped anchor in Jamaica, so I have some idea about how
the anthologies are organised. I listen to the contributing
writers talk about the communities that make up this city—
Eastleigh, Kilimani, Pangani, Westlands—and the dark-
nesses that stalk these streets. The moderator, a woman who
seems genuinely enthusiastic about the collection, asks the
editor, Peter Kimani, about the police who feature in several
of the stories and not often in a positive light. Peter smiles
his familiar soft and knowing smile. He does not yet know
I'm in Nairobi; I've come here tonight partly to say hello
to him. Peter shrugs, "This is Nairobi. We all know what
the police mean." And then he looks into the large audience
for confirmation. "We all know, don't we? Let's test this—by
show of hands, how many people here actually like the
police?" From the packed house, only one hand is raised in
the air. I can only see the hand. I do not see the body to
which the hand is attached, and yet the hand is so very
noticeable in this place. It is noticeable not only because it
is raised but also because it is white. *Who here actually likes
the police?* Only one hand. Only a white hand. And everyone
laughs knowingly, nervously.

Dear Binj,
    I hardly take pictures in Nairobi, largely because it is the
law of the city and I don't want to risk arrest. And because
a long time ago I read Sontag and it stayed with me—these
ways that the camera can come between ourselves and

experiences. I therefore do not take a photo of the man standing in the middle of traffic on Kenyatta Avenue, his dreadlocks piled high on top of his head, but wrapped with a turban. He is wearing a white pufferjacket striped with red, gold and green, and across the back is emblazoned: "JAMAICA". The taxi driver points this out to me and says "Yes—those Jamaican colours are very popular." He asks me about Rastafari and the dreadlocks hairstyle, which he says is now so very popular with Kenyan youths. And I think what an incredible feat this is that my small island has pulled off, how thoroughly we have taken these things and made them our own, that a Kenyan taxi driver would not associate the colours red, green and gold with his neighbouring country, Ethiopia, and he would not associate dreadlocks with his own people—the Maasai or the Mau Mau.

I never asked you about the short dreadlocks that you occasionally sported—what they meant. I didn't ask you because it would have been a stupid question—the kind of question that often came to me, and that often annoyed me in those days when I too wore dreadlocks. It is as if our hair has to have some deep meaning or an entire philosophy attached to it. But I think maybe people ask about the meaning of our hair because it is easier to ask that than to ask about the meaning of our entire bodies.

You rocked so many styles, Binj—completely bald, short dreadlocks, a bright red swish that looked suspiciously like a Nike logo, stripes of bright blue, half bright purple and half pink, all these colours not usually imagined on bodies like ours. I loved that about you. I still do.

Dear Binj,

I was told about Rosslyn. I was told it is a whole other world, almost as if you are no longer in Nairobi, but I do not accept this. I think it depends on what you expect of cities, and what should we expect of cities if not contradictions? Still, there is a noticeable shift driving from the city centre to these suburbs. The gates of Rosslyn lead to long driveways and the houses are set so far back that you cannot see them. Out on the street, before I turn into the art gallery I have come to visit, I pass a white woman walking her dog. She raises her hand above her head to acknowledge me and I do the same—but her hand reminds me of the one that was raised the night before. *Let's test this—by show of hands. How many people here actually like the police?*

It is in Rosslyn that I first hear the local word for the thing that happened to me two nights before—or that almost happened. I turn into the long driveway; I walk past the house set far back, past a paddock for horses, through a sculpture garden and finally inside the art gallery. I end up talking to two other white women who are gracious and kind and have offered me tea. They raise their eyebrows when I tell them what hotel it is I am staying at, so close to the city centre. "Well," says one, "you had better brace yourself for what we call a 'Nairobbery'. It is sure to happen."

A Nairobbery—so common to the landscape that it has its own name, like an indigenous flower. I imagine the "nairobbery" as a dark hibiscus. I do not admit to the women that I have experienced it already. It was already attempted. It is as if I want to protect the reputation of the nameless boys who almost harmed me. Instead I shift the conversation and ask the women about their accents. One woman looks at me a little surprised. "England," she says, as if it should have been obvious—and it was. I realise I haven't been clear. "I'm sorry," I say, "I meant where in England?" "Oh," she says, understanding at last. "I'm from Devon. But I've been living here for ten years."

The other woman, the one who owns the gallery, says, "Well, I was actually born here!" And she says it with what seems to be an equal mixture of defensiveness and defeat. This is a fight she has both won and lost already. She has won it because she is still here; she has lost it because she always has to explain. There is, of course, a whole world of things that cannot be said, and certainly not over tea, and not in light of the kindness she has offered me—but an entire history all the same that explains why she could have been born here, and why she lives in a house set so far back from the road, and why she speaks with an accent so untouched by the country she claims, as if her accent, like the house, is set far back from things.

Binj, I think about this neighbourhood—Rosslyn, and another that I had visited some days before—Karen. Not Kilimani, or Kileleshwa, or Kawangware, but Rosslyn and Karen. Neighbourhoods that may as well have been named after the women with whom I am speaking—were in fact named after women like them—where women such as these can walk their dogs and be less afraid of the nairob-beries that bloom like hibiscuses against the sidewalks of this city. Or simply less afraid of Nairobi.

And sipping the tea, I think about all these things that cannot be said over tea.

Dear Binj,

I take the Nai Nami tour. The reviews of it are excellent and it isn't expensive. Nai Nami—my Nairobi. A different kind of tour, done by former street boys. I think about the dangers of this kind of tour—not physical danger, but maybe something spiritual—how we make tourist products out of other people's poverty. I still go on the tour, but I try to keep this danger in mind.

I arrive at the meeting point a little early but still expect to see a group waiting. I do not. Exactly at the appointed time, a young man with short dreadlocks walks up and scans the faces around. I suspect he is the guide and I suspect he is looking for someone white. I'm suddenly too shy to tell him it's me—just in case he isn't actually the guide. He is looking at his phone and so I send a WhatsApp message to the tour group chat they added me to the night before. He looks up then, directly at me and walks over smiling. "I'm sorry, first I thought it was you, then I thought no, he's Nairobi, and then I wasn't sure."

I take a strange comfort in this—that he thought I might actually be from this place. "Is it just me?" I ask.

"Yes . . . sometimes we have as many as eighteen, today it is just you."

We are joined almost immediately by another guide. I am outnumbered two to one—more guides than tourists, but I think it is better this way. We do not walk as if on a tour, but like friends walking through their own city. They are as interested in the fact that I am from Jamaica, and from Kingston, as I am interested in their Nairobi. We do not go into the pretty buildings, not that there are many of these in the centre of the city. The historical landmarks are only pointed out if we happen to be walking by them anyway. Instead, they show me a police officer discreetly accepting a bribe from a motorist. They pause to shake the hand of a security guard in front of a store and then tell me his story—that he was once a wanted gunman, but he disappeared for several months and everyone thought he was dead but now he's returned with a new passport and new name—but it's him and there he is working as a security guard. They show me the corners where they once slept in those days when they were homeless, and where was warm but unsafe because you could not see anything—you could not see what was coming, and where else was cold and uncomfortable but provided a better vantage point from which to see the authorities who occasionally came to "clean the city".

They ask me about Vybz Kartel and Mavado and the Gully and Gaza war in Jamaica. They have gotten things mixed up though—turned them the wrong way around. They think Kartel represents "Gully" and that Mavado represents "Gaza". "No no!" I tell them laughing. "It's the other way!" Later, I understand the mistake. As we walk by an elaborate canal system into which the city drains itself, where all the rubbish of Nairobi sails when it rains, they point out that there was a group of homeless boys who actually lived in these gullies. They were quite a ruthless gang and Vybz Kartel was their hero and so they called themselves the Kartellos. I tell them that in Jamaica the gang of homeless boys who live in the gullies has a slightly different reputation. They lean in to listen but I do not have the heart to explain any further. Masculinity can be such a fragile thing.

Or maybe I am not giving them enough credit. One of them asks me about the tattoos on my arms. I explain that they are barcodes for the books I have written. "You are a writer?" he says.

"Yes," I answer.

"Like Binyavanga Wainaina?" he says. And it takes me by surprise—your name suddenly in the air.

"Yes," I say, "like Binyavanga."

"I read a story about him," the boy tells me, "but I think he's dead now. Yes. He has died."

Dear Binj,

I envy you this—that you were able to come back home. I have thought about returning as well. I have been thinking that my time in England is drawing to a close and that I would soon go back to Jamaica. I even thought this is the year it would happen. I even applied for a job at the university there. My father asked me if I was sure. My friends asked me if I was sure. Had I really thought it through? My cousins asked me if I was sure. My old mentor, who I asked for a reference, asked me if I was sure. I was so sick of everyone asking me if I was sure, and had I really thought it through and all the implications? In the interview—this was just a couple weeks ago—every question from the panel was a version of "Are you sure?" Sometimes it was asked nicely, as if with genuine concern, and sometimes the question had an edge to it—almost combative. They told me I was overqualified so did I really want this job? And at this institution? And for the first time I really did begin to wonder if this was what I wanted after all. Return is a much harder thing than I had imagined it to be.

Dear Binj,

It is my last night in Nairobi and I go to a one-woman show. I sit under a tree with a carving of the word "Karibu" swinging from it and think about how this word has bookended my trip. The storytelling show isn't very good but there is love in the audience. The storyteller has managed to bring out many of her friends who are here to cheer her on. At the beginning she encourages us to laugh as loudly as we feel to laugh, and at the sad points—because there will be sad points, she tells us—we can cry ugly tears if that is what we feel to do. But there is little in the art of her stories, in the telling of them or the structure of them that would provoke much laughter and certainly not enough pathos to provoke tears. Still, at the smallest opportunity the audience laughs as loudly as they can and it feels they are performing as much for her as she is for them. And I love it. I love that she is loved. I love all the love that is in the room.

Long after the show is over, I stick around. Some of your old friends are here—Zuks and Parselelo and Hana. We are ordering glass after glass of red wine. We are tipsy. Now we are telling our own stories, and we are laughing and we are crying, and Binj—this is the thing—every other story is about you! Parselelo raises his glass and says "To Binyavanga!" We all raise our glasses. We do it again five minutes later, and every time there is a story about you, we raise a glass to you.

I did not know you were dying. I only sensed, from afar, that something had happened. Something had shifted. It was as if you were unspooling. Online, everything you said seemed explosive, sometimes irrational. Parselelo says it seemed to him that you were trying to say everything that needed saying, to confess everything that needed confessing, to do everything that needed doing, to upload your giant brain and all its wonderful thoughts to the world, like a legacy. From afar, I did not understand this. It all seemed so erratic—so compulsive.

I am here. It is almost a dozen months and a dozen strokes too late. You are already gone, and you are forever here. You are forever in this place that you did finally write about—this place to which you brought your body back.

12

SOMETIMES, THE ONLY
WAY DOWN A MOUNTAIN
IS BY PRAYER

K enya shares its longest border with Ethiopia—779
kilometres—a more or less horizontal line, but jagged
enough that it doesn't seem, at first, like the arbitrarily straight
lines that Europe drew up and down all over this continent—
lines that often ran across villages, or across a single family's
compound. Where one country ends and where another
begins is not always neat or clear, though politics and walls
and border police increasingly make it so. Still, it is possible
to cross the border from Kenya into Ethiopia by car or even
by foot. Moyale, Fort Banya and Omorate—all are possible
entry points. A successful crossing depends on a few things—
obtaining, from Nairobi, a forward-dated exit stamp in your
passport, obtaining a police permit, and having the good for-
tune to meet gun-toting authorities on either side of the border
who are in good and generous moods. I had briefly contemplated this, wanting some parts of my trek across Africa to be
literally that—a trek—but it was not worth the headache.
Instead, I get to Ethiopia by a plane and by a prayer.

About the prayer, I will say this—some habits die hard. I have found it easier, over the years, to give up on religion—the whole idea of it and the practice of it. It has been easy for me to do this when I consider religion's history and also its present—so much of it bloody and hateful, so much more damage to be found there than nourishment. I have given up on Sunday mornings in Jamaica, on the hard pews, on the choirs, on the dodgy dogmas and the dodgy preaching, on what often feels to me like a shallowness of thought met by a depth of zeal. It has been easy for me to give up on religion, but harder to give up on the idea of God. Maybe it is this—that as a writer I spend so much time talking to myself, trying out sentences, it is a relief to sometimes direct that never-ending internal dialogue to something else—someone else out there who could be listening.

No. It is more than that. I am only trying to make sense of my contradictions. You see, on days when I am alone in my flat (I don't know why I should find it embarrassing to admit this), I play Gospel music, and loudly. I play songs by Tasha Cobbs Leonard or Kirk Franklin—the kind of song where the lyrics are simple but whose power comes from the repetition of that simplicity; the kind of song that builds and builds into a magnificent tearful crescendo. And in those moments, certain that I am by myself, my body behaves in the way that it has always behaved in the middle of such music: I close my eyes, I mouth the words, my hands sway above my head. The body often betrays you like this. Sometimes my body betrays the fact that I am not quite the atheist I sometimes pretend I am.

I almost miss the flight from Nairobi to Addis Ababa because of my own carelessness, so the prayer became necessary. I had been told that I needed a visa to enter Ethiopia and that I should do this online at least a week before travelling, my Jamaican passport offering me unvisaed entry to few places in this world. I did not apply for the Ethiopian visa because I had also read that it was possible to simply get a Visa On Arrival. This was possible not with my passport but with the British Residency Permit I also held. At the airline desk the agent checks her computer and says *no, no—it is not possible. You have read the wrong information! It cannot be done. You need to have been issued an electronic visa before boarding the plane.* She is not being unnecessarily difficult; she has tried more than once to check me in, but the computer keeps on saying NO. This is when I begin to pray.

In the corner of the departure lobby, a man has set out a mat facing east. From that mat he is rising and falling and rising and falling and chanting. My prayer is not as extravagant, but I believe it is as earnest.

I go online to apply for the visa. They need a passport photo. I find a white wall and take one with my phone. They also need a picture of my passport. I take a picture of that too. I send in the application. I send a follow-up message, a desperate note about my flight being in just one hour, and whether there is any way the process can be sped up. I add another line about prayer, as if sounding pious might win me points with whichever bureaucrat is on other end of the email.

I do not know if it is the prayer that works, or if on Saturdays they are just extremely efficient at the Ethiopian Visa

Office, but in half an hour my phone pings with a new email. My visa has been issued. I am able to board the flight for Ethiopia and I choose to believe it is at least partly the result of prayer.

I am only in Addis Ababa for a night so decide to make the most of it, but it takes me a while to leave the hotel. I have become overly suspicious. Cautious. It is a residue from the shock of almost being mugged in Nairobi. It seems, even to me, like a trauma I haven't earned. What if my body had not been male, or had been smaller? What if I had in fact been mugged, had been hurt, and still had to go back out into the world like so many of us have been hurt and have had to go back out into the world? I wonder if I would have had the strength—the courage?

At the elevator, a man dressed in a red uniform asks me for my room number and I hesitate. "Why do you need to know?"

"Because you are only staying a night," he tells me. "So that we can give you a wake-up call in the morning."

But I do not trust this. I am suspicious of everything. I am wary that a random worker should know exactly how long I am staying and want my room number just as I seem to be leaving. I tell him I will arrange with the front desk for the wake-up call, but thanks. Paranoid, I sit in the lobby for a while. I replay the conversation. I return to my room and transfer everything important to my hand luggage, I hoist it onto the top of the wardrobe and push it into the corner where it cannot easily be seen. I say a prayer and I finally leave.

I had been told by the driver who dropped me to the hotel and by the staff in the lobby, that this is a safe neighbourhood. When saying this, both the driver and the staff in the lobby had pointed towards the UN building. "See! The UN! Yes, very safe here."

Right outside the hotel, boys are trying to stop the passing cars, asking for money. There is nothing threatening about them. They are speaking with pretend-Jamaican accents and they find their own performance very funny. I find it funny too. I walk past them. I have decided that after walking around for a bit, I will take a taxi to the famous Addis Mercato but I've only gotten a few hundred feet into my walk when Haile strolls up to me. Observing him, I wonder if he is a priest—there is a quality of kindness to his face, and a wooden orthodox cross hanging from his neck. The crisp blue cotton shirt he is wearing, however reads to me as "bus driver" or "tour guide". Haile is polite enough, but I am still so wary of these encounters. He says he saw me at the hotel and I nod, but he doesn't seem to be going anywhere, walking step to step with me. I decide to ask him where the nearest coffee shop is, hoping it is somewhere along this street, that I will be able to duck in while he walks on. This proves to be a mistake.

"Yes, yes . . . coffee," says Haile. "We make great coffee here. I'Ll take you to a good coffee shop." And now he has attached himself to me, guiding me through lanes and streets to what he promises is the best coffee shop around. It is a local shop and seems well patronised. Sitting on low seats, he takes out his wallet, and from that wallet a card—an official

ID of sorts. His name really is Haile, and he is indeed a tour guide. Registered. He wants to assure me of this fact.

I make a second attempt to ditch him, though I am half-resigned to him being my tour guide for the day. It's OK, I say to myself. I usually resist these kinds of things, but what's the harm in giving in to it just for one day? I ask him how to get to Addis Mercato and he says, "Yes, yes, we will go to the market now." He gets a taxi and gets into the passenger seat while I sit in the back. On the way we pass by what looks like a church and the driver and Haile are making extravagant but silent gestures towards it—a prayer—as if their bodies do not know how to pass by something so sacred without performing this ritual. I will see this many more times in Ethiopia. We pass by a large compound, the fence impressively tall and on two posts of the gate are mounted bronze lions. The Conquering Lion of the Tribe of Judah, I think, and at the same moment, interrupting but confirming my thoughts, Haile says, "it is the palace of Haile Selassie. The first palace though. There is a much bigger one that he built. It is very, very important that you see that." He is already planning a tour for me.

It is not long before we stop. It seems the Addis Mercato is not so far away as I thought it would be. The taxi driver says he will wait—it is no problem, and Haile ushers me into a store that is the usual kind of tourist trap, selling all the kinds of souvenirs that I can never bring myself to buy. I try to smile politely at the shopkeepers who are fawning over me and showing all the cheap items probably made in China. I smile and say no thanks, no thanks. No, I am just looking.

I give it just enough time that I think is polite and then walk away to explore other shops. "But why you don't buy?" a woman insists before I can fully exit. I just wave my hand. Haile asks as well, "You don't want to buy?" And I say, "No, I just want to explore the market." "Oh?" he says, as if surprised by this. "You want to go to the market? OK we will go now." "So this isn't the Addis Mercato?" I swallow the tinge of annoyance. It's OK. It's OK. I'm saying the words to myself like a mantra. I'm just going along.

We get back into the taxi and actually head to the market this time. I know why I don't like being guided, why I hate being literally pulled this way and that, having to walk ahead when it is I'd rather stop and explore, or else having your guide pounce on everything your eye happens to catch, saying "Oh! You want this? I will get you good price!" I know that Haile means me no harm. It is a hustle. That is life here.

I explore Addis Mercato—supposedly the largest on the entire African continent. The building in the centre of the market is a remnant from the Italians—but from that epicentre the market sprawls impressively in every direction. The streets seem to go back for miles. The lanes are packed and as you walk through them women keep on grabbing at you— "Please just look!" But like every market it is often just the same things again and again—knock-off clothes in one area, men hawking belts which they snap over and over in their hands, asking you to feel it. "Genuine leather!" they say, and snap it again. "Genuine leather." Other areas sell sets of those small cups without handles in which coffee here is usually served. In other areas there are scents for incense, and every spice imaginable.

I do not linger much at any stall. Haile is hovering. Otherwise he is walking briskly and I am following. Sometimes he pulls me and it feels a little rough. "Yes, yes, I have to protect you," he says. "Hold your phone tight!" he says. "Hold onto your money," he says. "This way," he says, even as he is pulling me and I swallow the urge to snap and say, "Yes I'm following but stop pulling me! I don't like it!"

On the way back Haile is telling me what we will do tomorrow and I feel no guilt about the fact that I am lying to him. I have arranged to meet him at a time when I know I will be well on my way to Awassa, and from there to Shashamane—the Rastafari settlement. Soon he is talking to the taxi driver in Amharic and I look out the window. I get so used to the background hum of their speech that even when some sounds seem to make sense in English, I dismiss it as just the random accident that happens between languages. "Fat ass. Fat ass!" Haile is saying. It takes me a moment to realise that he has switched to English and is speaking to me again. We are stuck in traffic and he is pointing to a woman walking on the road. She is large and beautiful, walking with a kind of swag I associate with women from my own country. "Fat ass!" he says again, "So fat! Not Ethiopian. Nigerian I think. There are so many of them." I do not know how to respond. He then says before going to the hotel we should stop at this lovely bar. There are women there, he assures me. He winks. Nice women. Not prostitutes. Nice women. Ethiopian college students. I decline. I tell him I am tired. At the hotel I pay the taxi and give Haile the rest of my money for his trouble. "Tomorrow?" he says.

"Tomorrow," I agree. But tomorrow I will be in Awassa.

This is a true story: an American woman once stood outside the gates of Windsor Castle, about to go in for the tour. She was standing with a man, more than likely her husband. They wore matching wedding bands tight on their thick fingers. There was, in this moment, a plane flying overhead. Windsor Castle is very close to Heathrow Airport and the plane was coming in for landing. It was low enough that you could even read the writing on its belly. EMIRATES. The American woman looked up, shook her head, and then she tutted. She turned to the man and said, with a contempt as heavy as her Southern drawl, "Now who would build a castle in the middle of a flight path!?"

I am not sure why I think of her as I stand by the lake in Awassa, except I wonder what she would make of this place and its palpable history, so palpable in fact that it feels deeper than mere history; it feels like the history of history.

I have felt this before—in Jerusalem and in Egypt and in Iraq—though it was easier in these places to locate that sense of the ancient. It was in Jesus's tomb; it was in the Pyramids; it was in some artefact of stone pushing its way up through the sand. It is not so easily located here, though it seems to touch everything, even the rust of modernity—zinc fences, forgotten sandals, Coca-Cola cans tossed to the side.

Earlier, on the streets of Awassa, we drove slowly as one might in the highlands of Scotland because sheep had clustered in the road. Here, it was a herd of cows that we had to slow down for while a man wrapped in shawls waved a stick and shooed them to the other side. And something about this felt as if I had slipped back to the beginning of time. The birds here are as tall as men. They walk the streets, these marabou storks, and there is something so majestic about them, and also, something terrifying. Their beaks are big and powerful, like a pair of machetes. Some people call them the nightmare birds. I feel certain they could kill a man. Here, at the lake, they fly against the setting sun while the hippos bathe on the other side.

In Binyavanga Wainaina's essay "How to Write About Africa", by which he really means, how NOT to write about Africa, or how to write about Africa, badly—he says with caustic irony, "the African sunset is a must. It is always big and red. There is always a big sky."

Only here, at this lake, do I find his tongue-in-cheek advice difficult, because the sunset really is big and red, and the sky really is the biggest sky I have ever seen. And the acacia trees around the lake are beautiful. And everything feels like every word he warns us against throwing at this continent— timeless, primordial, ancient, holy. I remember the American woman and briefly wonder what she would make of this, or if she would even know how to make something out of it— standing here, unable to see either castle or plane—only the birds, and the hippos, and the water, and the big red sun in the big wide sky.

* * *

For centuries people have been coming to Ethiopia to find God—to find the thing that they have been praying towards. My people have as well. They came to Shashamane.

I would have been disappointed in Shashamane had I not already had some idea of what to expect—not a thriving Rastafari metropolis—a vision of Mount Zion, but instead, a somewhat broken dream, a place where a prayer might come to die. Rastas from around the Caribbean had left the outskirts of one society only to join the outskirts of another. This is what happened: in Ethiopia there had been a revolution, and then there was another. Haile Selassie's generous land grant to anyone of African descent in the Caribbean who wished to return "home" was rescinded. To date, none of the Rastas have received citizenship to Ethiopia, but still, it was OK. They had this town. They had Shashamane.

In the early days there were over a thousand Rastas here. It was a small town, but they outnumbered everyone else. Things have changed over the years. A major road now runs through the town that isn't so small. The population doubled, and then it tripled, and then it quadrupled—multiplying over and over again. Shashamane's population now stands at over 100,000; the population of Rastas has dropped to under 700. To be on the outskirts of Ethiopia was one thing; to end up on the outskirts of Shashamane itself is another.

And yet, there is no regret here—no sense that a wrong decision was made. Thomas is my guide. He pronounces it in its original Amharic way—Toe-mas. His features are distinctively Ethiopian but his accent is distinctively Jamaican. Only sometimes at the edge of it do you hear the Amharic underneath. I ask how it is that he perfected the accent to a place he's never been to. "Yu done know," he begins, "De I did grow up wid a Rasta elder and yu just pick it up after a while. And is dat de people dem waah hear who come fi tour, yu know. Mi naah pressure nuhbady hard, yu zeet. But a my hustle dis, suh mi haffi learn di talk."

He takes me around, knocking on the few gates dotted about where the Rastas still live or worship. He warns me away from the Twelve Tribes Headquarters, however. "Yeah de vibes dere not nice any more. Mi nuh tink you woulda like it. De elders dem get old, suh dem not dere fi keep the livity. A just some young eedyat bwoy who a try hustle a money. Yu zimme." I believe him, and trust him, and find it sweet that he doesn't see the irony—young boys just trying to "hustle a money". We end up at Bolt House—a Jamaican restaurant. Outside, along the wall that encircles the restaurant is a kind of mural—Usain Bolt is in the middle of the mural, and posing in the middle of a Jamaican flag, Haile Selassie is on the far right, Bob Marley on the left as well as the Lion of the Tribe of Judah. Inside, I meet Sister Joanne and later her husband, Brother Desai, a Twelve Tribes elder who leads the very same Headquarters we did not get to. Brother Desai smiles widely when he hears that I too am from Jamaica but frowns deeply when he asks what it is that I do and I confess that I am a writer.

"I don't trust writers!" Desai says gruffly. He is not being impolite, but he does not seem like a man interested in politeness if it came to that. I nod. I get it. He continues, "Writers are a dangerous set of people. Dem only want to write the negative things. The sensational. And dem don't want to tell people the truth about dis great Africa." And it seems to me that he is talking from experience—that there are specific writers he is thinking about. I do not know what to do other than nod again. I wonder how many writers and journalists Brother Desai has come across in his forty-four years of living here—how many have sat before him with their tape recorders waiting for him to tell them again the story of the Rastas in Ethiopia. How many times has he read back a portrait of himself that he does not recognise? Would he recognise himself if he read this that I am writing now?

"What month you born?" Brother Desai asks, and I tell him, October. He looks me up and down. "October. Hmmm. You know what you are led by? The backbone." He reaches a hand behind himself and runs a finger along his own spine. "Listen, this is not horoscope. Rasta don't deal wid horoscope. Dis is de ancient wisdom dem did try to hide from we. You are led by the backbone. Balance is your ting. Balance is what guide you." And I don't know why this should have made me feel so unsettled, so exposed, as if this complete stranger has looked and understood something very true about me, as if his ancient wisdom is true. I put my hand to my chest and bow. "Blessings, Elder," I tell him. "I'Ll take that."

Desai talks for a while longer about the evils of Babylon and the greatness of Africa, but I am only pondering his early words. "Writers are a dangerous set of people."

In Lalibela, the mountains are monasteries and the rocks are churches; the holy places never built or constructed in the way we usually think of buildings or constructions. Rather, they are dug into the landscape, or chiselled and carved out of the boulders. It is breathtaking to stand in these places and contemplate the work done, to have carved out from a single rock an entire church! This is Africa's Jerusalem—or at least that was the intention, to make a holy place on the continent so that the early Ethiopian Christians would not have to risk their lives pilgriming across hostile territories to get to the real Jerusalem. So many hundreds of years old, and these churches are still in use. On any given evening sitting in Lalibela, it might sound as if the rocks and the mountains are chanting.

I go up the mountain with Prince as my guide—Prince who grew up here in Lalibela, who studied biology at university and used to teach in a high school, but the money was too little. He makes more now as a tour guide. Climbing up, the mountain is especially loud. It is the Day of Emanuel. We reach and I wander about. Even in the midst of the solemnity and the worship, an argument develops on the mountain. Prince is involved. It takes me a moment to realise I am implicated as well. We are standing in the doorway of one of the worship spaces. A man is sitting on the floor in front of the priest, his camera out and the full zoom of the lens pointing at the priest. So this man, sitting down and trying to take his picture, has turned around, visibly annoyed by us. "Could you come further in!? You're blocking the light!" Prince does not move. He would have to squeeze himself into a corner to accommodate the man trying to take the photograph. When I realise what is happening, I stand firmly with

Prince. The man is trying again to take the picture, but whatever he sees in the viewfinder is obviously too dark. He throws his fists in the air and turns to us again. "Could you get out of the damned doorway!?" He is almost frothing with rage. Prince does not move and I am standing firmly with Prince. And then Prince can no longer hold his tongue. "You are selfish man, sir." He says. "You come here, into holy place, and command people, make people uncomfortable. You are selfish!"

Two English women are standing behind the sitting man, and in a fluttering, flustering kind of way they are suddenly tripping over their own mouths to speak. "Oh no, no, no! He wasn't making us uncomfortable at all!" They protest. I assume by "people" they could only understand Prince as referring to them, as if he too is not a person in this place, as if he could not possibly be speaking on his own behalf. "Yes," I say to the women, adopting as much of a British accent as I can conjure, "but it is rather impolite, don't you think—to come to someone's country and be so rude about things—to bark orders at them like that? Don't you think?" And they look at me, seemingly stunned, not sure what to make of me. "Yes, I suppose," one says. "I was just trying to defuse an argument." I do not say the obvious—that in trying to defuse the tension, they instinctively came out in defence of the rude man—the man who has now picked up his camera in a huff and stormed out.

Prince's hands are now a flurry of activity—his finger constantly going from forehead to chest, then shoulder to shoulder, making the sign of the cross, the way that Haile and the taxi driver had been making this gesture on my first day in Addis Ababa. "I'm so sorry." Prince says to me. "I did not want to start an argument in a holy place."

He seems embarrassed that he has possibly offended me, but even more, that he might have offended his god. I do not know about God, but I try to reassure him that I am not offended.

"That man was Italian you see," Prince says, as if that should explain something else, and it does—the complicated history between the two countries and these ways that tourism often replicates colonialism—the outsider who feels the native should show deference, should happily squeeze themselves into corners when commanded, but who could never contemplate, yet alone tolerate, bodies such as ours—dark bodies—visiting any of their European cities and making such demands.

We walk out of the temple. The Italian man is there at the door waiting on us. He is still obviously bothered. He needs to get something else off his chest. As if he has not already revealed his full self, he looks to both of us and says, "You people should be grateful that people like me visit your country! You people should be thankful that we are pouring money into your economy."

You people. I have been included. Because of my body. Because of my skin I have become Ethiopian and worthy of his contempt. He cannot imagine someone like me being similar to himself. He cannot imagine me as the tourist. *People like me*, he had said next, by which he meant white, though I suspect he is not fully aware of all that he implied. I am seething. I am so very angry at this Italian man who thinks Ethiopians must all obey and grovel before him; I am angry at the English women who seem to only understand themselves as people; I am angry enough to say something. And I wonder, how do we do it? How do we make it through each day when there is so much in the world to be angry about?

Prince has ignored the Italian man. He has simply walked ahead. I follow him, skipping from stone to stone and climbing higher up of the mountain. Prince stops and takes a seat. I sit away from him, understanding that he maybe needs a moment.

The sky is so very large and the mountains are still chanting and the landscape spread out before us is holy. I look over to see that Prince's eyes are now closed and his lips are moving in prayer.

13

MY BROTHER, MY BROTHER

To hear him speak it, every man here in Ghana is K's brother. "My brother, my brother" he says, a linguistic embrace, a claim of kinship, and when K does this—when he pronounces that word "brother", there are no rolled Rs and no highland lilt. He loses, at once, all traces of his usual Scottish accent, an accent that at times could seem peculiar to his body. Instead of the Scottish accent he would have learned at school and from his friends and from the world around him growing up, he draws for the other accent he would have heard in his household—West African sounds. Nigerian to be specific. "My brudda, my brudda," he says. K tries to secure local rates of entry at the Wli Waterfalls and at the monkey sanctuary and clutches his heart as if mortally wounded when they charge him, as they do me, the tourist rate. "But am I not your brudda?" K asks with wide and hurt eyes, and though they both laugh at this, slapping each other as men do on their shoulders—that slightly-too-loud laugh that often happens between customers and service providers that reveals the entire interaction as false, scripted—there is a hurt unsaid in all of this: *No, sir. I do not really consider you my brother.*

*   *   *

I too could claim brotherhood here. Given another history, this is the country to which I would have been born. Or if not to this country, then at least to this landscape. The same history that took my ancestors away is the same history that drew the borders and invented a single country out of a patchwork of ethnicities. It is the same history that created sudden brotherhood between Ashanti and Ewe and Konkombo men. Look, said some English governor, you are all brothers now! You are all Ghanaian. But which of these are my actual brothers—I do not know.

There are so many things I do not know, not even the seasons, and it worries me. It is always important to know the seasons. I was just about twenty years old and at a writing workshop in Trinidad. I must have blithely said something about enjoying the summer not knowing then that the word "summer" slipped easily off the tongue of a Jamaican but not so easily off the tongue of a Trinidadian. The tutor, a fiercely bright writer and activist who still had shrapnel in her bones, mementos of a revolution she had helped to fight on another island, looked at me over the rim of her glasses. "Summer!?" she gasped? "Allyuh in Jamaica have summer now? And I suppose you does have winter and autumn and spring too?" Funny—I would actually defend the Jamaican use of "summer" now. I would say, But isn't this what we have always done—taken language, hollowed it out and then refilled it with our own meanings? We remade the language for ourselves. But I also heard her loud and clear. Yes, it is important to know the seasons. It is important to describe a place and its seasons on its own terms.

Here, it is the harmattan—a season I have never felt or witnessed before. It is nothing like spring, or autumn, or summer, or winter. And neither is it anything like the Caribbean's dry seasons or our hurricane seasons. The harmattan is its own thing. The sky is nowhere to be seen, as if Nyame has taken his entire lodgings elsewhere, off on his yearly God-vacation. The sun is an orb shining dimly behind what feels like fog. It is as if a huge thunderstorm is building, except there is no moisture. The air is dry. You feel it in your chapped lips. What I mistook as fog, I understand now is the tiniest particles of the Sahara Desert. The whole thing feels like a landscape of dreams. My brothers are always coming out of, or disappearing, into mist. It is weird when I realise I too must always be doing the same. I walk about trying to take note of this season I have never before experienced. The time of the desert in the sky; the time of the low sun; the time when we go along as if entering or exiting dreams; the harmattan.

I do not know the languages here—not Ga or Ewe or Nzema—not a single one of the over seventy indigenous tongues, not even Ashanti Twi, though I know much of my own Jamaican patois borrows from the structure of that language. And can I really be a brother in this place if I do not speak a language from here—or if I can only speak to my brothers in the language that separated us from each other?

In Kenya and in Ethiopia I had felt a tinge of embarrassment, but the feeling wasn't unlike the way I have felt in France—that shyness of not knowing a language, of having to be accommodated, of having to sheepishly ask, "English?" In Ghana the feeling is much larger than just a tinge. It is a profound hurt. And sometimes it is as if I really ought to understand what is being said, as if I really could if I just concentrated enough, if I tried a little harder to remember something I must have forgotten. At the market, a woman with mangos crowded between her legs calls to me, "babarima" —son. And then she says something else I do not understand. I smile and say, "English?" and she stands up from her mangos. She looks me up and down, her arms akimbo, and then makes a sound, deep and guttural, "Eh!!"

I say "Sorry."

On her face is a look of scorn, but it is as if she is looking not at me but at something behind me. It is as if she is saying, "But really, what kind of a mother is this, who has taken this boy to be raised in another country but never taught him his mother tongue? Now look at him! He has come back, so big and worthless, yes? So big and worthless. But he cannot even speak to us. Eh! What kind of mother is this?"

And I think, oh maame, if you just replace that word "mother" with "history" then you would be correct. For really, what kind of history is this?

In the streets of Accra the men are hawking their goods—carvings and cheap touristy paintings and bags and shirts and shoes all with Kente designs. They call to me. They call me "brother" but with extravagantly affected black American accents, as if they are in Harlem or the Bronx. "Yo ma brother! Whassup!? Come here and look!" I walk by but cannot avoid the man who, free from the confines of a stall, approaches me—one hand dripping with leather necklaces, the other covered with T-shirts. "Yo ma bro!" he says to me, "Why don't you buy some o' my Authentic African shit, man." I observe him for a while, stone-faced, the silence just long enough to make the veneer crack a little. "But why do you speak to me in an American accent?" I ask. Now the mask slips completely. "I am sorry my brudda," he says, "I am just trying to sell these things." And I love this moment, how without the pretence the distance is reduced a little between us. I look at his things, still doubtful that I might buy anything. "But where are you from then?" he asks me. "Jamaica," I answer. And he smiles brightly. "Ahhh but see! You are still my brother!" re-establishing both a brotherhood and a distance between us.

We go to Elmina Castle. I feel it is something I have to do, because I have imagined for so long this "Door of No Return", this precise place where so many of my direct ancestors— great-great-grandfathers and great-great-grandmothers— would have crouched their malnourished bodies under, would have squinted at the first direct sunlight they had seen for months, and would have boarded the boat that was the beginning of a terrible amnesia, would have taken them away from everything they knew. To return then to this place where no return was ever expected, ever imagined—to walk the opposite way, from the beach and to the door and through it—is something, a kind of healing perhaps—a way to say, *I am so sorry that I do not know your names; we have forgotten so much. I only know that I am from you and that you were here, and that my body is the legacy of you. So I bring you back; I bring you back inside my own body. Look, look! You are finally home.*

The tour begins in the dungeons. About twenty of us follow the guide. I know that this experience will be meaningful, but I do not expect it to be emotional. I am generally not built like that. I already know what to expect from this tour but I am still not ready. All my reading has not prepared me for the actual smell of it all, how more than a trace of what happened here should still linger after so many hundreds of years. And the air around is suddenly so thin. I feel some part of myself slipping—a feeling I have never felt before— and I realise if I don't concentrate really hard, if I don't push my entire consciousness into every part of my body—my toes, my elbows, my ears—I will faint.

I linger behind, allowing the tour to walk a bit ahead. K comes over to ask if I am OK, and I can only lift up a hand, unsure what that hand might communicate but knowing that if I opened my mouth to speak I would only start sobbing. K seems to understand and leaves me alone. I take a few deep breaths and then am about to join the group again in the next room when a couple return to the room I am still in. It is a white couple. They smile politely at me and then the woman places herself against one of the walls, extending her neck and smiling brightly. "Here, John! Right here!" she instructs the man as he focuses his camera, and it takes all my willpower not to grab the camera and smash it to the ground.

Twenty minutes later and we are all back outside in the sunlight. The tour guide is recapping for us some of what we saw down in the dungeons and pointing to the chapel where we will head to next. He lets the group walk a little and then comes over to me. "My brother," he says. "Are you OK? Would you like to do this tour without . . ." and he does a gesture that makes me smile, a gesture I have grown up my whole life knowing. He points with his lips. He does not say "white people"—just the gesture, but I tell him it's OK. I'm OK.

Of course I am not completely OK, but I think my feelings are more layered than I know how to sort through. I feel a sudden profound disappointment in everything—in history. I am disappointed in the white woman who felt a slave dungeon was a great backdrop for a picture of her wearing her biggest smile. But my disappointment extends even towards the tour guide. It is not fair, what I feel. I am disappointed in a history that we had no part in playing—a history that our bodies merely inherited. Still, there is a reason that I was born in the part of the world to which I was born, and a reason why my guide was born in Ghana. It is the reason why when he approached me and said, "My brother," I felt a hollowness in the words.

Isaac is behind the wheel and we are driving back. I am riding shotgun and K is sprawled out on the back seat. It is evening but I only know this because we have been out all day, and also the time on the jeep's dashboard tells me so. If it was only for the harmattan, every part of the day would look the same, like dusk—like we are driving through a never-ending fog. We almost fail to see the police flagging down our vehicle. At the last minute we pull over.

The police—and it is a large group of them, many more than the usual pair I am used to seeing on Jamaican highways—seem weary and agitated. I know the look; I have seen it in Jamaican police officers on highway duty. They have been at this spot for too long and have not issued as many tickets as they had hoped to, and more importantly, have not collected as much bribe money as they had hoped for. One officer,who seems to be in charge, gestures for Isaac to roll his window down. *What is your name? Where are you going? Where are you coming from? Where do you live now? Where were you born? Are you sure—I know this village. Are you from there? I can call people to check. Make sure you are telling me the truth!* The questions seem unnecessarily aggressive to me, and fast—one on top the other, as if he wants Isaac to trip up on something—make a mistake. Isaac's politeness is practised and efficient. The officer tells him to get out of the car and bring his documents over. Isaac disappears into the group of officers while another officer tells me to wind down my own window. "Who are you?" the officer barks.

"I am Kei," I answer. I know this game well enough. I have played it in Jamaica. My answers will be efficient, precise. They will be polite but with an edge of curtness.

"What do you do, Mr Kei?"

Brother Desai's words come back to me in this moment: *Writers are a dangerous set of people!* And indeed, in this moment, it would be a dangerous thing to be a writer. I know that this is a negotiation of power but it is important in such moments to always remember your own power is never greater than the officer's. You must be humble. If possible, you should give an answer that makes you seem adjacent to power. You must give the officer the impression that, if it comes to it, you are the kind of person who will be able to call upon people. In these moments, I am never a writer. That is not an answer that works in these situations. Instead, I give another truthful answer that is more helpful. "I am a university professor," I say.

"Oh?" says the officer, "Do you have ID?"

I do not, but I have my bank card, and I show him, my title written on it.

"We are sorry to inconvenience you, Prof.! It is just a standard check."

I nod.

The officer has paid no attention to the back seat, but on his own K is winding down the window. "Hello, my bruddas! My bruddas!? How are you doing?" he calls out brightly from the back seat and I think to myself, *Oh shit!*

Outside, the officers have become even more agitated—almost desperate. All of Isaac's documents check out. Everything is in order. His registration is up to date. There is no easy misdemeanour to pin on him, no easy bribe to extract. They have now ordered him to open the back of the jeep so that they can do a search.

Unsurprisingly, the officer who was at my window is now ignoring me in preference for the man he has found in the back seat, so much more enthusiastic—so much more willing to talk. "And what are they searching for, my brudda?" K asks.

"Drugs and weapons," the officer replies, "but only illegal weapons. We have no problem if your weapon is registered . . ." he lets his sentences trail off, dangling, as if hoping K will pick up the threads.

"Oh," remarks K, "So it is OK if the weapon is registered?"

In the front, I shake my head. I wonder why is he engaged in this conversation. Why would he ask for clarification about weapons when we have no weapons?

The officer continues, "No you can have a registered gun. But no drugs. Drugs are illegal . . . no marijuana, no cocaine."

"No drugs?" K asks.

"No." The officer is smiling.

I know that K is not so naïve as to think these officers mean us any good, but he is naïve about other things. He is naïve enough to believe in the good logic of law, and in the basic rights of citizens, and that there are simple things we can do to protect ourselves and to hold the police to account. These are the kinds of naïve beliefs you might have if you grew up in a place like the UK or even the US. You understand that the police might often do unjust things, but you believe that you will be able to shine a light on that injustice —to amplify it and bring them to account. You would not believe such things if you grew up in a place like Jamaica or Ghana, and I realise then that there are so many kinds of kinship in this world.

It is because K grew up in Britain he believes in the good logic of law and in the basic rights of citizens and does not think anything of taking out his phone and filming the officers as they search the back of the car. He does not know that less than a year ago, Ghanaian police assaulted the journalist, Malik Sullemana, for daring to film them. Everything had happened the wrong way around: it was a police officer who had crashed into the vehicle in which Sullemana had been riding; it was the police officer who tried to flee the incident like a criminal. Sullemana caught up with him and confronted him, but then when other officers arrived on the scene it was not to offer justice to Sullemana. When they realised he was filming the whole thing, they beat him up badly. They left him with blood clotting in his left eye, bruises on his left arm, and swelling in his left leg. If all that wasn't bad enough, they then threw him in jail. And K does not know that less than a year before that incident with Malik Sullemana, the same thing had happened to Latif Iddrisu. It is illegal (and the logic of this would not make sense to K) to film the police in Ghana, and whether this law is written in the actual books or not is immaterial. It is a law the police will defend with all the brutality of their muscle.

The officers do not find drugs in the jeep because there are no drugs in the jeep. They do not find weapons in the jeep because there are no weapons in the jeep. But the officer now sees that K is filming on his phone and he smiles as if all his patience has paid off and all his Christmases have come at once.

K is ordered out of the car and frogmarched towards the group of police. I know he did not handle this well, but I feel sorry for him. It is such an intimidatingly big group of officers and they are wearing a range of uniforms—from solid blue, to khaki, to various shades of camouflage. Some of them are holding guns and others batons. They are all shouting and gesticulating and K is in the middle pleading. I feel sorry for K, but there is nothing I can do. I turn on my phone to finish a crossword puzzle. Words from the argument drift over to me. "Illegal!" shout the officers, and something about "social media". K is protesting, "But I'm a foreigner! I'm just a Sco'ish lad! I don't know your rules!" And despite myself I have to stifle a laugh—how suddenly all attempts at brotherhood have been abandoned. We are always choosing between our various identities, occupying the one that suits a situation best.

Isaac is visibly worried. He is constantly moving between the jeep and the officers. Whenever he returns to the jeep, he has his hands on his head and says "Oy-yoi-yoi! This is bad. This is so bad." I must seem so heartless to him; I only raise a brow and go back to my crossword.

An officer comes to my window. "We are sorry, Prof.," he says to me, "we know you are a good man. We respect you. But your friend. Oi! You know what it is like, Prof. These people, they come into our country and they take these videos," he is talking to me as if I am suddenly his brother—as if I understand this world, which I do, and as if I am sympathetic to his position, which I am not. "Oh yes, Prof.," he continues, "they take these videos and then they write all manner of things—blogs and essays. Yes. That is what these people do. They write these things, you would not believe. And they make us look so bad!"

"Is that so?" I ask, and can't help but marvel at his logic. Why wouldn't it occur to him that if they did not do bad things, maybe bad things would not be written about them? But such logic belongs to another landscape.

"Oh yes!" he assures me. "The things they write about us—especially on social media. On that Facebook! It is terrible. We cannot allow it." I nod. I go back to my crossword.

The confrontation seems to stretch on forever. The officers are shouting, "Illegal!" and, "Social media"! Isaac is pacing back and forth and saying "Oy-yoi-yoi!" K is pleading—"just give me back the damn phone and I'Ll delete it!" But the officers refuse. "It is evidence!" they say. "We cannot delete evidence!" These are the words they use, but it is not what they mean. What they really mean is, *how much money will you pay us to let this go?*

Another officer comes to my window. "But Prof.," he says, "Why do you not intervene?"

"And what could I possibly have to contribute?" I ask.

He looks at me for a few seconds and then shrugs. But I know what he wants. He wants the whole situation to get even more chaotic. He wants to have us all emotionally involved and desperate. He wants us to be panicked about the possibility of K going to jail so that we will reach deeper, much deeper, into our collective pockets. He does not understand—or maybe he does—that my refusal to get involved is its own act of resistance.

"I'Ll just wait here till you're all done," I say, and he walks away a little defeated.

No headway has been made in the brouhaha and there is now only one option for the officers. They must make good on their threat. They have to up the ante and show their muscle. K is ordered into the back of the police jeep. Isaac is told to follow as they take him off to jail.

We are back on the road. Isaac keeps saying "This is bad, this is sooo bad," but this whole farce of an arrest seems ridiculous to me. It is not an arrest. We all know. This is a shakedown. A mile into the drive and the police have pulled over to the side. They've all climbed out to repeat the same performance as they had done before, but perhaps now having proven a willingness to go through with their threat. They are still shouting, "Illegal!" and, "Social media!" but now they have added something else to make their intentions more clear. "It is such a pity we have to arrest you," they say to K. "If only there was something else we could do. If only there was another way to get out of this mess . . ."

They will go no further in spelling out the bribe. It has been put on the table for us to take or not. Isaac talks to the officers and talks to K. An amount is agreed. We scrounge up all the money we have between the three of us. The transaction is made. K is released.

The drive back is even more silent than it had been before. K is brooding in the back seat. His disappointment is thick in the car, but a disappointment that cannot be easily named— like a sort of betrayal, like the darker truth of brotherhood. "You OK?" I ask, and K nods, but he does not meet my eyes.

14

AND THIS IS HOW WE DIE

I knew what it meant to be white and I knew what
it meant to be a nigger, and I knew what was going
to happen to me. My luck was running out. I was
going to go to jail, I was going to kill somebody or
be killed.

—James Baldwin

Dear James,

I saw your death. Not the one that found you in Paris, the cancer eating away at your stomach, but rather the one you fled—the one you said would have come to you if you had not left America.

James, this is how you die: you are twenty-five years old. You are a young man with a fine and muscled body. Perhaps it is partly the blessing of good genes but also the result of discipline. You have trained your body. You often jog through the coolness of a Georgia morning. It is February and though winters in this part of Georgia are already mild, you are glad that the worst of it is over, but the humidity has not yet crept back. What a fine thing it is

191

to run. How uncomplicated. No machines, no crowd of men in Y-back T-shirts grunting as they lift bars of iron over their heads. It is just the road and your own feet pounding its surface, your heart racing to a speed it is used to. You do not think about your breath the way beginning runners do, the ones who worry they will run out of it, who stop and bend over with their hands on their knees to catch the thing they fear they will lose. But you, James— you take your breath in your stride, literally, filling your lungs with the cool air, the cool air oxygenating your whole body, your beautiful body running against your own time.

There is a jeep. It is behind you. At first you think nothing of it. You do not think it contains danger. You only pull to the side of the road and wait for it to pass, but it doesn't, and it is only then—this refusal to pass, its insistence on staying behind you that you begin to worry and that your heart begins to race even faster than the speed it has grown used to. The driver is calling for you to stop. *Stop,* he says. *Stop! I need to talk to you!* And you wish that you had worn earphones whether music was playing from them or not, but at least you could have pretended that you did not hear him.

There are trees on the side of the road. You think about running into the greenery but just as quickly dismiss the thought. You would be stuck there. You would be hiding like a frightened criminal. You have done nothing wrong. You are only jogging—running now—and you do not know why the man in the jeep behind you is shouting for you to stop. It makes sense to stay on the road, to simply do what you have been doing. There is the possibility someone else will appear on the road, and just like that, someone does. Another jeep is stopped ahead of you—a white pickup truck with a man standing in the bed of it. The driver's door is open and the driver is standing outside. They do not seem like men who you would run to for safety. They are big and burly and bearded and white. And they are loading guns. Why are they loading guns? Not the neat kind of handgun you might tuck into the elastic of your shorts, the metal pressed cold against your back— but those big-ass rifles that you have to pump. A white man's gun, you think. A gun for a modern confederate soldier. What seemed like it could have been safety has now revealed itself as an even greater danger.

It is no longer such a fine thing to run—not when you are running for your life, not when you really might lose your breath and never regain it. Your heart is pounding so much faster and harder than your feet on the asphalt. You cannot turn around. The other jeep is still behind you as if to block you in. You pull closer to the white jeep and then pull sharply to the side deciding to run around it. The men are shouting. *Stop! I told you to stop, boy!* In front of the jeep the man points his gun towards you. Fast as you run you cannot outrun a bullet. You imagine the bullet in your back and decide the only thing to do is to pull the gun away from this man so intent on killing you. You run towards him and try to wrestle the gun away. There is an explosion. Your ears ring. Your wrist feels as if it is on fire but there is no time to think about the pain. You reach for the gun even more desperately. You both stumble even as the man tries to reload the gun. Another explosion. Now it is your side that is on fire. And why? What is the cause of this? You struggle some more. The man reloads. A third explosion. You feel like your whole self is on fire now, like the brightest light is spreading out from your own stomach. You fall. The man says, *Fucking nigger*. And James, this is how you die.

This is also how you die—

You are twenty-six years old and it is a Friday night. There is nothing particular about this night, nothing special except maybe it is a little more quiet than usual. It is as if the whole world is holding its breath, which it is. It is strange to exist in this time, in the held breath of the world, but if you had to give your own feelings a name just now, you might say you felt content, even safe. It is the end of the week and you are in your own home, in your own bed, and your head is rested against the broad chest of your own boyfriend. Somewhere in the distance you hear a siren and for a moment your body tenses, not out of fear, but as if to ready yourself for work.

You used to work on ambulances—the screeching siren following you to the old woman who has collapsed in her living room—a heart attack, or to the couple trapped in the metallic crush of a car that has skidded off the highway. Now you work in the emergency room and the sound of sirens is the sound of work coming in. But you are not in the hospital; you are at home, in your own bed, with your own boyfriend, and the movie playing on the TV is more watching you than you watching it. You have both decided to stay in tonight because of that tension that is out there in the world. Though the State of Kentucky has not yet declared a lockdown (that will happen in three days) the strange virus that is already bringing the world to its knees is close. It has already entered this bluegrass state, this Commonwealth of Kentucky. You have been thinking about your own safety, of course. How could you not? You have wondered if your job will provide you with the right gear, face shields and gloves. You are an essential worker, after all. That comes with risks. You are the kind of woman who considers the risks. Your mother has said as much, her hand soft against your cheek and her eyes wet with a thing like love. *You've always had your head on straight, girl. Always.* But risks are for tomorrow. Now—just now—you are home. The terrible virus is out there doing its thing in the world. For just this moment, you are allowed the feeling of safety.

The banging at the door causes you and your boyfriend to jump, to scream a little. It is so sudden. It is so loud. It is so insistent. You both jump out of bed, fully awake and terrified. Your boyfriend marches into the living room. He has taken out his registered gun like a man protecting his castle. This isn't his home, but you are suddenly glad he is here tonight. *Who is it?* He is shouting. *Who the fuck is it?* You are shouting, even as you cower in the hallway. Your boyfriend points his gun towards the door—the door that is banging so loudly as if all the tension that was out there in the world is now gathered right outside your own apartment trying to burst in. And then something you have never seen before—the door flies off its hinges and into the room like the big bad wolf just huffed and puffed and blew it out of the way. Your boyfriend fires the gun but you hear so many more shots. So many gunshots. And your body as if it is on fire, as if the brightest light is spreading through your entire being. And James, this is how you die.

This, again, is how you die –

You have bought Marlboro. There is a warning on the box. *Smoking Kills. Smoking Leads To Reduced Lung Function.* You are so used to these warnings that you have stopped reading them. You did not recognise the man behind the cash register. No. Not even a man. A boy. He had tilted his head back to look up at the full height of you, and then on the double-headed eagle tattooed in black ink across your chest, much of it visible because you are wearing a sleeveless muscle shirt. The boy has thought about getting his own tattoo—but not yet. His father would surely shout at him. His mother would surely cry, Allah, help us! We did not come to this country to have our boy become a common gangster. And a tattoo as large as yours would have taken up his entire torso. You have gotten the cigarettes and the change from the $20 note you handed to the boy.

As you walk out of the store you are tapping the box of cigarettes against your forearm. You are not sure why you do this. It is just a habit you picked up when you were just a teenage boy in Texas. The older men did it with a kind of nonchalance that seemed to you manly, almost sophisticated. Some smartass told you there is no need to do this again—that it had something to do with the way cigarettes were made back then, filterless, and loose tobacco could end up in your mouth which wasn't at all pleasant. This tapping was in order to "pack" the cigarettes, but it is not necessary these days. You do it anyway, a sort of ritual.

Stop! Stop! You turn around. The boy is running towards you with a green bill in his hand. It is the $20 you handed to him. He stops before reaching you as if his courage is fluctuating. Is he more afraid of you or the boss? *This money is no good! Give me back the cigarettes and the change and take this back. It is no good.*

You have learned a long time ago to pick your battles, and this is not one worth fighting or even responding to. You almost smile at the boy. On another night, if it wasn't for this damned virus bringing the world to its knees, you would still be working at the club and it is a boy like this who would have come to the door and handed you his counterfeit ID. He would have squared his shoulders back, tried to man up, tried to look you in the eyes in the way he imagined a man would, trying not to show how scared he was. You wouldn't have had to look at the ID to know that it was fake—just the boy and all his tremulous youth showing and you'd have to decide one way or the other. If you let him in he will do so happily, but if you shake your head, hand him back his ID and gesture towards the streets, he would turn around immediately and leave without question. In no situation will this boy fight you, so you smile at his useless demand, turn back around and continue towards your car holding the pack of Marlboro with the label *Smoking Kills*. And, *Smoking Leads To Reduced Lung Function.*

You do not know how many minutes have passed. You haven't gone anywhere. You are sitting behind the wheel of your car talking with your friends. You jump a little when there is a sudden tapping at your window. You jump even more when you turn around to see it is the police. *Open the door!* he yells, so you open the door, and you are tripping over your own words to be polite and to be respectful, to say *Yes sir*, and *Yes, Mr Officer*, but also—what the hell? What's happening? What have I done? And so quickly, in the midst of all your flustered words and your fumbling, the police officer has reached for his gun and you are staring down its barrels and he says PUT YOUR FUCKING HANDS ON THE WHEEL! You do it, and you start to cry because you have imagined this so many times—you have experienced this so many times—and you wonder if today will be that dreaded day. Will you die by a policeman's bullet? *Please don't shoot me*, you manage to say. But no, James. That isn't how you die. Not by a policeman's bullet. It hardly matters though, because this right here—this moment—this is how you die.

They have pulled you out of your own car. They are trying to shove you into the back seat of another. The air is suddenly tight around you—the world an unbreathable thing. You are afraid of the airlessness. No. You don't want to go into the back seat of their car. You are trying to be polite, to say yes sir, and yes, Mr Officer, but you also want to know why? Why the fuck is this happening? But everything is fucking this and fucking that and do what you're fucking told and put your fucking hands up or put your fucking hands down or put your fucking hands behind you. You are on the ground now. Your lips kiss the asphalt. Your hands are behind you and in handcuffs. You can't go anywhere or do anything, but the policeman's knee is on your neck. This is what you say: *Please, I can't breathe.* They pay as much attention to that as they have to everything else you have said. Your words do not matter. How do we make our words matter? You say it again. It is ignored again. You say it twenty-two times. It sounds like this:

Please, I can't breathe.
Please, I can't breathe.
Please, I can't breathe.
Please, I can't breathe.
Please, I can't breathe.
Please, I can't breathe.
Please, I can't breathe.
Please, I can't breathe.
Please, I can't breathe.
Please, I can't breathe.
Please, I can't breathe.

Please, I can't breathe.
Please, I can't breathe.
Please, I can't breathe.
Please, I can't breathe.
Please, I can't breathe.
Please, I can't breathe.
Please, I can't breathe.
Please, I can't breathe.
Please, I can't breathe.
Please, I can't breathe.
Please, I can't breathe.

And then you say something else. *Momma. Momma!* But your mother is already dead. Two years now, almost to the day. You say Momma, like you are speaking to what is not there, or to what is there and cannot be seen. You say Momma like the spirit of her has come down to meet you at this crossroads, is kneeling before you as if to offer you water, but she only puts her hand under your chin like a pillow and says, *It's OK, Slim.* This is what she has always called you. *It's gonna be OK. You coming with me.* And this is how you die.

Dear James,

I have seen my death as well. This is how I die:

I in one ah them lil cars—a Nissan Tiida—the kind you does see on every road in Trinidad these days. I with two ah my pardners and we driving along Juman Drive in Morvant. The road not so busy like it could be. It have a terrible virus out there like it come to kill the whole ah we. Dr Rowley lock down Trinidad tight, tight. You can't fly in; you can't fly out; you can't buy doubles on the side ah the road; you can't even lime with the fellahs in a bar at night. And unless is bread you out there trying to get for yourself or your children, they say you shouldn't be on the road at all.

Just so, we see these three big police jeeps—no flashing lights, no sirens wailing or nothing, but they coming down the road hard hard hard like is them alone and God on it. My pardner who driving wonder if he should pull the Nissan over into the ditch cause is like them police boys ready to knock we off the road and into eternity.

I say out loud, *Look trouble now!* cause dem fellahs only drive like this when they have evil on their minds. This right here is trouble heading towards a set ah people who before long going to find themselves on the wrong side ah these boys' batons, or worse, their guns, and only if we lucky we might read about it in the papers tomorrow. Imagine, I barely get these three words out my mouth when the third jeep pull up hard in front ah we. The other two jeeps that already pass screech to a halt behind we and the police boys jump out with these guns big like maybe they think is the Taliban they fighting here in Trinidad. They shouting, *Come out! Come out with your hands up.* I could piss myself right then and there.

Look, when them fellahs give you instruction—it don't matter how it unreasonable, it don't matter how it unjust, it don't matter that maybe is just a Saturday night and they having their fun trying to humiliate you, you does do it! You do whatever they ask so that afterwards you can walk home. Some ah these police boys, is like if they don't pull a trigger they feel they don't do a day's work. You can't give them the opportunity.

We so frighten and so chupid we trying to open the car doors with we hands already up in the air. We had to stop. Take a breath. We open the car doors. We push we hands out immediately, up, up in the air so they could see we not holding anything. We pull the rest ah we bodies out the car and stand up, under we arms wet with perspiration. I don't know how it happen or why, but I standing there with my hands in the air, and my pardners standing there with their hands in the air, and just so, just so, I hear bang, and then bang, and then bang, and I feel something like a fire, like a bright white light ripping through my whole body. I look to see my two pardners going down to the floor. I wonder why they would make joke at a time like this. Why they would lay down on the ground at a time like this? Except I thinking I want to lie down there with them. And this is how I die.

This is also how I die.

I so vex it hard to talk or keep things straight in my head. News come that police kill three ah dem boys. Our boys. The police say they had guns. They say the boys had opened fire on dem and there was nothing they could do but to fire back and kill dem. It was a shoot-out, bullets flying everywhere, and they say is just luck and training that make it that none of the police fellahs was injured. Not a graze, not a nick, not a nothing. Well, that is what they want us to believe.

Evil does make you chupid and careless cause the police don't notice that the shop by the side ah the road where they stop the Nissan Tiida had its own CCTV camera on the wall, and the camera film the whole thing. So we watch. We watch and we see how the first boy had come out ah the car with his hands up and the only thing he holding onto was his own fingers, his own life. So how all of a sudden gunshot start to fire? How all of a sudden the three boys end up on the floor dead?

So we say we goh lock down Port of Spain. We goh burn things! We goh mash up things! We goh march and shout. We goh demand justice. We goh demand answers! We goh carry on until the commissioner he own self come down and talk to we like we is people with we own eyes that can see things, and we own intelligence that can make sense ah things but can't make no sense ah what happened on that road in Morvant.

I not only marching for myself but I marching for the boychild who ent born yet—who been growing inside me these past eight months. I don't want him to born into a world where he could catch bullets in he stomach just so, even when he follow all the instructions; he could catch bullets just cause a police fellah feel he should catch bullets; just cause he black and he poor.

It have a set ah people in this country right here who from the other week when they kill that fellah George

Floyd in America, been jumping out their whole selves to say Black Lives Matters and to say they standing in solidarity with their brothers overseas, who marching to the US Embassy here to tell the ambassador that we here in Trinidad tired ah the foolishness that does happen every day in America. But like black lives only matter if they live abroad, or if they have money, cause this same set of people now staying home and asking why we out in the streets causing bacchanal and why we should vex when is just a set ah criminals that the police did kill? Sometimes when you think through things like this, you wonder if it even possible to ever find the words to explain the foolishness ah this world.

So we marching. Me with my eight-months' pregnant self marching too. The police all around us telling us to stop it. They telling us to disperse and go home. They telling us we in the middle of a pandemic and we putting lives at risk by congregating and it come to me clear clear right then that I live my whole life in the middle of a pandemic. Every day is a risk. Now the police like a set ah bullies with a set ah bullhorn shouting how the demonstration illegal. Shouting how they might have to lock up the whole ah we. *Go home*, they say. *Allyuh is a set ah hooligans*, they say, as if is only bad behaviour and not understanding or accepting your place in the world that could cause you to stand up and say, *We is people too. Treat us better, nah?*

But you know these police fellahs. Some of them feel if they don't pull a trigger they don't do a day's work. One ah them decide if we ent goh listen to the sound ah he voice, we goh listen to the sound ah he gun. He fire a couple shots. Bang. And bang. People decide for true is time to leave this spot. They start to scatter. They start to run. I want to run too but is like I feel a sudden fire going through my whole body. I feel it for myself and I feel it for the boychild who ent born yet. And I say to the boychild inside me, *in a lil while we will go home, but leh we just lay down for a moment on this road.* And this is how we die.

And James,

Every day it is like this in America. And in Trinidad. And in Jamaica. And in this whole world. We write because there are always things we have withheld. We die because things have been withheld from us, which is to say, respect; which is to say, dignity; which is to say, love.

BIG UP

To the most extraordinary agents: Harriet, you are such a blessing to me; Alice, you keep on making magic possible.

To the kind of editors a writer only ever dreams of having— Ellah Wakatama at Canongate and Elisabeth Schmitz at Grove Atlantic—editors who both trusted me and pushed me. This book became something better because of you.

To Melanie and Rochelle and the Renaissance One crew, who have been so patient and have made my life as a writer possible these past couple of years.

To those vagabond writers and thinkers who are my tribe, and in whose company I grow: Marlon James (dude!!!), Leone Ross (keep on rocking it!), Garnette Cadogan (yu nuh fraid dem lock yu up?), Annie Paul (you little trailblazer, you!), Malika Booker (the carnival essays are for you), Ronald Cummings (look how far we coming!), Yvonne Weekes (thank you for adopting me), Jason Allen (J'ai hâte de lire tes poèmes) and Tanya Shirley (girl, you sooo wrong, and always so right!).

To Leila and Vahni and Alex and Phillipé, my Trini family.

To Jean Binta and Dona and Jonathan and Matthew, my UK family.

To the family that chose me—Shauna, Richard and Natalie and Jude and Zane. Mom, we continue to miss you. And Dad—the original Kei. You guys are my life and my fortress.

And of course, to Dionne Brand, who I haven't yet met, but whose fierce and moral writing teaches me how to think.